Paul Reid

August 1933

Lehighton Penna.

THE UNIVERSITY OF CHICAGO PUBLICATIONS
IN RELIGIOUS EDUCATION

Edited by
SHAILER MATHEWS   THEODORE G. SOARES
W. C. BOWER

———

HANDBOOKS OF ETHICS AND RELIGION

This series of Handbooks is intended to set forth in a readable form the results of the scientific study of religion and ethics. The various authors do not undertake to embody in any detail the processes which lie back of their conclusions. Such technical treatment is more appropriate for works of a strictly scientific character than for those intended not only to be used as textbooks and collateral reading in colleges and theological seminaries, but also to be of help to general readers. The volumes all seek to conserve the values of past religious experience. While each author is free to present his own conclusions, the entire series has the common characteristic of historical method. The editors have not prescribed any rigorous uniformity of treatment, but believe that the individuality of treatment will serve to stimulate thought and discussion. It is hoped that the series will help to show that the method of experiment and criticism contributes to stronger religious faith and moral idealism.—THE EDITORS.

THE ORIGIN AND GROWTH OF THE HEBREW RELIGION

THE UNIVERSITY OF CHICAGO PRESS
CHICAGO, ILLINOIS
—

THE BAKER & TAYLOR COMPANY
NEW YORK

THE CAMBRIDGE UNIVERSITY PRESS
LONDON

THE MARUZEN-KABUSHIKI-KAISHA
TOKYO, OSAKA, KYOTO, FUKUOKA, SENDAI

THE
ORIGIN AND GROWTH
OF THE
HEBREW RELIGION

By

HENRY THATCHER FOWLER
*Professor of Biblical Literature and History
in Brown University*

THE UNIVERSITY OF CHICAGO PRESS
CHICAGO, ILLINOIS

TO
PROFESSOR FRANK CHAMBERLIN PORTER, PH.D., D.D.
OF YALE UNIVERSITY
UNDER WHOSE GUIDANCE I FIRST TRACED IN ORDER THE
HISTORY OF THE HEBREW RELIGION THIS BOOK IS
DEDICATED WITH MUCH GRATITUDE AND RESPECT

PREFACE

The present volume is designed to offer a guide
for study rather than simply a new essay or treat-
ise upon the history of Israel's religion. The
principal source book for this field of investigation
is the Old Testament. It is intended that those
using the present textbook shall go to the sources
to discover the facts for themselves before they
read the discussions in the following chapters or in
the books suggested for supplementary reading.

The student should make written memoranda
of the facts gathered from each group of references
given at the opening of a chapter, and only after
this has been done should he read the chapter itself.
In this way he may become an independent worker
who gathers the facts for himself and tests the
conclusions of others by his first-hand knowledge.

If the time devoted to the course of study per-
mits, the student should compare with the material given in each chapter the parallel discussion in
one or more of the authors assigned for supplementary reading, and should then write his own
account. A suggested list of headings for such
an independent history is given in Appendix II.

TO THE TEACHER

Teachers who have not been accustomed to
send their pupils to the Biblical writings to gather
data may be surprised to find that even superior
students will at first report far-fetched inferences
rather than the plain facts contained in a given
passage. With practice and guidance they will
usually learn, after awhile, to find the definite
points pertinent to the topic under investigation.
Working together in the class will be of service at
the outset, but this should not be allowed to take
the place of independent work for too long a time.

It does not fall within the scope of the present
volume to discuss the order of growth of the Old
Testament. The general order adopted as the
basis for tracing the history of Hebrew religious
ideas and practices is indicated in the brief chrono-
logical table of Hebrew literature, following the
list of principal dates in Hebrew history, at the
opening of the book. Reference is made in Appendix I to several of the standard works that discuss
the literary history of the Old Testament.

In a history of Hebrew religion it is necessary
to use very frequently the proper name of the
nation's God in order to distinguish him from the
baals of Canaan or other deities recognized by
Israel's neighbors. Opinions may reasonably differ
as to whether it is better to use the familiar, though
incorrect, form Jehovah or the form Yahweh,

which probably represents pretty nearly the sound of the ancient Hebrew name. It seems to the present writer preferable, in a historical study of the origin and growth of the Hebrew religion, to use the ancient name rather than a combination of sounds that was never heard until more than twenty-five centuries after the time of Moses.

This handbook is committed to the use of teachers and students in the hope that it may prove a helpful guide in the inspiring effort to trace, in order, the upward course of God's revelation of himself through the succession of devoted and inspired teachers of ancient Israel.

HENRY THATCHER FOWLER

BROWN UNIVERSITY
February, 1916

CHRONOLOGICAL OUTLINE OF HEBREW HISTORY

Migration of Israel's ancestors from Mesopotamia, perhaps fifteenth century B.C.

Exodus from Egypt, *ca.* 1200 B.C.

Entrance into Canaan, *ca.* 1160 B.C.

United Kingdom under Saul, David, and Solomon, *ca.* 1040–940 B.C.

Kingdom of Northern Israel, *ca.* 940–722 B.C.
    Ahab and Elijah *ca.* 860 B.C.

Kingdom of Judah, *ca.* 940–586 B.C.
    Josiah's reform, 621 B.C.

Babylonian exile, 586–538 B.C.

Persian rule, 538–332 B.C.
    Rebuilding of temple, 520–516 B.C.
    Rebuilding of walls of Jerusalem, 444 B.C.

Greek rule, 332–168 B.C.

Maccabean age of independence, 168–63 B.C.

Roman rule, 63 B.C. to fourth century A.D.
    War against Rome, 66–70 A.D.
    Destruction of Jerusalem, 70 A.D.
    War against Rome, 132–135 A.D.

CHRONOLOGICAL OUTLINE OF THE HEBREW LITERATURE ESPECIALLY CONSIDERED IN THIS VOLUME

The beginnings of Hebrew literature (songs, hero tales, etc.) before 1040 B.C.

Beginnings of connected prose literature (stories of Samuel, Saul, David), before 900 B.C.

The great Judean and Ephraimite histories of antiquity (including the law codes of Exodus, chaps. 34 and 20–23), *ca.* 850–750 B.C.

The eighth-century prophets (Amos, Hosea, Isaiah, Micah), *ca.* 750–700 B.C.

Deuteronomy, written after 686 B.C., adopted as law, 621 B.C.

Zephaniah, Jeremiah, and Ezekiel, 626–570 B.C.

The restoration prophets (Isaiah, chaps. 40–66, Haggai, Zechariah, chaps. 1–8, Malachi), *ca.* 550–450 B.C.

Leviticus and the priestly history of antiquity completed and the Hexateuch compiled, by 400 B.C.

Job, Ecclesiastes, Chronicles-Ezra-Nehemiah, between 400 and 300 B.C.

Apocalyptic books (Daniel, Enoch, etc.), *ca.* 200 B.C. to first century A.D.

Mishnah, *ca.* 200 A.D.

CONTENTS

CHAPTER I

GENERAL SURVEY

References for study—

(1) Acts 17:22–31; Rom. 1:18–25; Matt. 5:43—6:34; Luke 4:16–27.

(2) Amos 5:25; Jer. 7:22; Exod. 20:24–26; Jer. 35:1–11; Num. 6:2–3; Amos 2:11–12.

Note in group (1) the questions discussed for Greeks and Romans which could be assumed as settled in addressing Jews; in group (2) the simplicity of Israel's early ritual and the protests against agricultural life.

I. SIGNIFICANCE OF THE HEBREW RELIGION

The great central beliefs of the Hebrew religion lie at the basis of the teachings of Jesus, Paul, and the others who had a part in the founding of Christianity. If we try to imagine how the work of Jesus would have differed if he had appeared in Greece or Rome instead of in Palestine, we can appreciate to some extent the significance of the Hebrew foundation on which he built.

In Palestine Jesus could assume that his hearers believed that there was one God and only one. When Paul spoke in Athens, he was obliged to meet the needs of those who lacked the Jews' perception of the spiritual Being who made the world

and all things therein; when he wrote to the
Christians in Rome, he discussed the folly of the
peoples who worshiped the created rather than
the Creator; but when Jesus spoke to the peasants
and fishermen among the Galilean hills or on the
shores of their lake, he could enter at once upon
the highest themes of God's character, purposes,
and will for man.   These hearers stood upon the
lofty ground of ethical monotheism, while the men
of other lands, even the most cultured lands, were
in the darkness of polytheism, worshiping beings
with passions like their own.

The advance of science with its revelation of the
essential unity of all things visible has now made
polytheism unthinkable among educated men, and
philosophy has found in man's moral capacities
reason for inferring a moral spirit central in the
universe.   But the humble men of Galilee to whom
Jesus addressed himself already believed that God
was one and that he was just and merciful.   They
believed this because they had been educated in
the Jewish home and synagogue where such faith
was the commonplace of instruction.

The classic nations with all their marvelous
civilization had not attained this clear vision, the
truth of which our modern science and philosophy
may help to validate.   When Paul went abroad,
as we have seen, he met those who knew no such
broad and inclusive religious views of life, but in

his own thinking and commonly in his arguments he started from the high ground attained in his ancestral religion and thence reached up and out.

The purpose of the present study is to trace the origin and growth of the religion that so sharply distinguished Israel from the other nations of the ancient world and made her one of the world's chief teachers.

Nineteen hundred years after the coming of Christ Israel's faith persists, in almost the precise form it had attained then, as one of the world's distinct religions, with some millions of adherents who have clung to it through every vicissitude. Out of this faith, with added elements and some vital changes, sprang Christianity; to Judaism and Christianity another great religion, Mohammedanism, owes its central doctrines of the unity of God and of his moral nature. To study the origin and growth of the Hebrew religion is, then, to trace back to its sources one of the most widespread and continuous streams of influence known to human history.

2. NEW POINT OF VIEW IN THE STUDY OF HEBREW CIVILIZATION

The decipherment of the Egyptian and Babylonian inscriptions, with the excavations and other researches conducted in Bible lands, has made possible a study of all phases of Hebrew history from a new point of view.

We now know Israel as a comparatively late comer in the truly ancient world of which she formed a part. We can see that she inherited much from the nations which had attained a high degree of cultural development a thousand or even two thousand years before there was a Hebrew nation. We trace back the history of the Tigris-Euphrates valley, whence the Hebrews believed that their ancestors originally came, to a time fully five thousand years ago, and the history of the Nile valley, whence the Hebrews believed that their ancestors came forth to accept Yahweh as their God, to a still earlier period.

The land of Canaan, where the tribes settled by the twelfth century B.C., there to be slowly consolidated into a nation, had been dominated by Babylonia for many centuries prior to 1700 B.C., so that the Babylonian written language continued in use there for many generations longer, though the political control of the land had passed to Egypt. For nearly four centuries preceding the Hebrew exodus from Egypt and settlement in Canaan the Pharaohs had held sway over the petty states into which the land was divided.

Canaan itself has yielded very little of early inscriptions, yet we are able to form a fairly clear picture of the Canaanite civilization which Israel found on crossing the Jordan and which she largely absorbed. References in the Babylonian and Egyptian inscriptions, letters found in Egypt that were sent from local governors in Canaan a few generations before the Hebrew settlement, recent excavations of old Canaanite towns—Gezer, Megiddo, Taanach—and references in the Old Testament writings have all helped to make this picture possible.

In the effort to get still farther back to the roots of Israel's life, her ideas and practices have been carefully compared with all that can be gathered from ancient evidence and from the customs of the tent-dwelling Arabs of today, who still preserve many of the religious usages of antiquity. These various lines of investigation make it possible to distinguish in a measure those elements in the Hebrew religion which are original and distinctive from those which were a part of the people's general heritage as a branch of the Semitic race or were borrowed from the Canaanites.

Our concern with those aspects of her religion that Israel shared with her neighbors and kinsfolk is incidental, since our chief purpose is to discover and trace the distinctive elements of the Hebrew religion. In these we judge that the secret is to be found of that which has enabled this religion to maintain its identity for three thousand years and to become, too, the basis of those two great missionary religions, Mohammedanism and Christianity.

Another source of the new point of view in studying the history of Hebrew civilization is the rearrangement of the Old Testament writings in the general order of their composition. Five generations of minute and painstaking study, in which the work of each scholar has been subjected to the most searching criticism and all available evidence has been constantly re-examined, have resulted in a general consensus of scholarly opinion as to the order of growth of the Old Testament writings. The positive results of this foundation work upon the principal sources for the history of the Hebrew religion will be assumed in the discussions of succeeding chapters. These results are briefly indicated in the table of "Chronology of Hebrew Literature" at the opening of the volume.

3.   ISRAEL'S HERITAGE

Consideration of Israel's inheritance must begin with the rejection of the idea, which has been widespread in recent times, that there is a primitive tendency toward monotheism in the Semitic race. Wherever we are able to get a glimpse of the most ancient Semitic life, whether under the simple conditions of the desert camp or in the rich cities of Babylonia and Phoenicia, worship is rendered to many beings.   Paton classifies the spiritual beings whom the early Semites worshiped, aside from their ancestor-worship, as: powers inhabiting physical objects, such as Ba'al-Shamem, "owner of the sky," Shemesh, "the sun," Sin, "the moon," baals of animals, trees, springs, mountains, etc.; powers presiding over departments of human life, such as Gad, "fortune," 'Anath, the goddess of War, 'Ashtar (Ishtar, Ashtoreth, Astarte), the goddess of reproduction; powers presiding over mental states, such as Gil, "joy," Wadd, "love." The first were known as baals, "owners"; the second were called by names expressing kinship or authority, brother, father, lord, or master; the third were styled spirits, as taking possession of man.

A prevalent tendency toward henotheism or monolatry, the recognition of one god for one place or tribe or nation, may indeed be observed among the ancient Semites as in early Egypt; but this belief generally tended to develop toward polytheism rather than toward monotheism. When one city in Babylonia or Egypt became politically dominant, its god assumed in the mind of the people a certain supremacy as a monarch over the gods of the conquered cities, whose deities were subordinated but not denied existence. With the development of kingdoms the confusions occasioned among the gods are hardly less perplexing than the mixtures in governments and peoples that arise from political conquest and absorption. If a new city with a hitherto insignificant god becomes supreme, it may be necessary to add to the god's proper name that of some god famous of old in order duly to glorify the upstart.

In the oldest and greatest seat of Semitic culture, Babylonia, such processes early mingled with other tendencies of religious growth to produce a most elaborate pantheon. In Egypt the course of theological confusion that had grown out of twenty centuries of consolidation of the nomes, each with its separate god, was temporarily interrupted by a royal monotheist about 1440 B.C. This Pharaoh, who styled himself Ikhnaton ("Aton is satisfied"), endeavored with all his power to stop the recognition of all other gods than Aton, the god of the sun disk. He even forsook his ancient capital, Thebes, and built an entirely new capital as a center for the dissemination of solar monotheism. Immediately after his death, however, Egypt returned to its old gods, and its religion became more and more debased in subsequent centuries.

While the religion of Israel may show some traces of Egyptian influence, it seems impossible to discover any direct connection between Ikhnaton's brief and abortive attempt to establish monotheism and the rise of Hebrew monotheism some centuries later. Whether or not Marti is right in regarding Ikhnaton's faith as purely intellectual in its origin, it did not spring from any such profound experience of the power of God within as that of the Hebrew prophets. The claims of the Egyptian sole god could be satisfied chiefly by reforming worship—a thing which could be accomplished for the time by the exercise of despotic power—while the claims of the Hebrew god, as set forth by the great prophets, were made upon the heart of man and required the transformation of all life. A study of the history of the Hebrew religion shows its monotheism to be the result of an inner development of the religion itself, not the externally imposed philosophy of any one thinker.

Although the great founder of Israel's religion and the people about him had come out of Egypt, their religion was established by their deliverance from the Pharaoh, and most of its inherited elements bear quite distinctly the marks of the Semitic culture of Southwestern Asia rather than that of the Nile.

The ancestors of Israel had been nomads from time immemorial, before any part of them were forced to taskwork in Egyptian city-building, and all indications point to the unchanging nomad ideas and practices as those that chiefly marked their life in the wilderness after the exodus. Many such tendencies persisted long after the adoption of agricultural and city life in Canaan.

Although the nomads recognize many spirits, they do not develop elaborate sacrificial systems. On pitching camp they may think it prudent to offer some propitiation to the spirits of the place and, on quite special occasions of festival or need, may share their feast of flesh with the tribal god, or make an offering to propitiate some offended deity, but elaborate sacrificial ritual with its stated offerings and libations develops with settled life. When Israel had long been settled in Canaan, great prophets decried the elaborate worship of their day, urging a return to the relative absence of offerings in the wilderness period. The early law, even after settlement in the land, permitted only a rude altar of earth or unhewn stone. We note first as Israel's inheritance from her nomad ancestors familiarity with simple, primitive forms of sacrifice in which many details of her later system were found in germ. She became familiar with a more developed ritual system among the Canaanites after crossing the Jordan.

Circumcision, which in later ages became so distinctively a rite of the Jews, seems to have been a general practice of the peoples in and about Canaan and of the Egyptians also; the Philistines, who had come into Canaan from the northwest, were distinguished from the rest as uncircumcised.

Mourning customs which persisted in Israel down to the time when she had attained her highest religious development are traced by modern students back to the times when men, in fear of the spirit of the deceased, sought by loud lamentations to frighten it away, or, by rending garments, throwing ashes on their heads, and mutilating their bodies, to render themselves unrecognizable in case the spirit of the dead man should return to its old surroundings. Even in modern Christian civilizations mourning customs are peculiarly persistent, so that we need not wonder if the rigid conventions of Israel in this matter were a part of her primitive Semitic heritage.

Many passages in the Old Testament indicate how natural it was for the Hebrews to associate the divine presence with such objects as stones, trees, springs, mountains. A stone might be set up as a beth-el (house of God), and the neighborhood of an oak or a spring was an especially appropriate place for a vision of God. The roots of such conceptions may be traced to early animistic ideas, in accordance with which the natural object was the abode of the spirit. The persistence of the association may be seen in Palestine and among the Arabs today. The spring or tree is still the shrine to which the people come in times of need to invoke the spirit of some deceased saint whose fame is connected with the place. Such sacred trees are often covered with bits of weather-beaten rags, fragments of the garments of petitioners who seek to come into communion with the saint's spirit and to obtain health, children, or other boon. These modern inhabitants of the land are Mohammedans, nominally monotheists of the strictest sort. Practically they seem to have more faith in local spirits than in the great and distant Allah. Such tendencies, which may be traced back to the nomad ancestors of Israel or the pre-Hebrew Semites of Canaan, explain much in Israel's religious history that has often been perplexing.

The simplicity of worship which was the people's nomad heritage was a part of the simplicity of all life that must always distinguish the denizens of the desert and its border lands from the neighboring city-dwellers. As the absence of elaborate sacrificial ritual characteristic of the days of wandering seemed to later prophets a true standard in reference to worship, so the rejection of all the refinements and luxuries of Canaan seemed to some religious reformers of later Israel the ideal life. Both the Nazarites, whom Amos counted as holy men sent of God, and the Rechabites, whose steadfastness Jeremiah chose as an example, refused to partake of the fruit of the vine, so characteristic of the agricultural life of Canaan.

The simplicity of life among the ancestors of the Hebrew nation was an ideal made winsome in the beautiful stories of the patriarchs, written at a time when comparative wealth and luxury had become prevalent. Idealized as these stories then were, shot through with moral and religious conceptions that belonged to a later age and were no part of the genuine nomad heritage, they were yet true to that inheritance in their loyalty to simplicity in worship and in all life.

The primitive Semitic nomad religion is not in itself characterized by the moral influence of the divine powers upon their worshipers, however much the memory of its simplicity might furnish a moral motive in a later age. Israel's conception of God's distinctly moral nature and demands is not even in its germ a part of her common Semitic heritage. It was not the Semitic race as a whole which attained and gave to the world the idea that the one God is in his essence moral. It is not because the Hebrew faith is the doctrine of monotheism but because it is the doctrine of ethical monotheism that it is of supreme significance in the history of civilization.

4. GENERAL OUTLINE OF HEBREW HISTORY

Before passing on from a preliminary survey of Israel's heritage from her early nomad ancestors, to a more detailed study of the rise and development of her own religion, it will be well to pass the great stages of the nation's history in rapid survey.

a) The pre-Mosaic period (before 1200 B.C.).— The Ammonites, Moabites, Edomites, and Hebrews

form the Hebraic group of Semites. The progenitors of these peoples seem to have moved down
southwesterly from Mesopotamia to the borders of
Canaan about the fifteenth century B.C. Ammon
found permanent settlement on the comparatively
well-watered and fertile lands between the Jordan
and the desert, Moab on the arable tableland east
of the Dead Sea, and Edom in the rocky fastnesses
to the south of the Sea. In the meantime it is
quite possible that some of the future tribes of
Israel made their way into Canaan, but the major
part seem to have continued a nomad life in the
regions to the south and not far from the borders of
Egypt. It is Israel's heritage from this stage of development that we have been chiefly considering.

At length a part at least of the progenitors of the
future nation of Israel, driven by need of food,
found its way across the border of Egypt and later
was forced into task-service under the Pharaoh,
Rameses II.

b) The Mosaic period (ca. 1200–1160 B.C.).—
Not far from the year 1200 B.C. those who had
been enslaved made their escape from Egypt.
Their leader in this movement, known as Moses,
had previously spent years among the Kenites in
the regions between Egypt and Canaan. The
people, uniting with kindred tribes who had probably remained outside of Egypt and with the Kenite
tribe into which Moses had married, waged suc-

cessful war with the Amalekites, another nomad group, and maintained themselves for many years with the fountain of Kadesh as their center. At length conditions east of the Jordan were favorable for an attack, and Moses led his people around the borders of Edom and Moab to the districts east of the Jordan. Here they succeeded in dispossessing the Amorites who, it would seem, had recently crowded the Ammonites away from the Jordan valley to the borders of the desert. A part of the Hebrew tribes made their permanent abode here to the west and north of Ammon.

c) *The settlement in Canaan (ca. 1160–1040 B.C.).* —The greater part of the Hebrews eventually crossed the Jordan and found settlement among the Canaanites; Judah with the Kenites and a remnant of the tribe of Simeon occupied that portion of the central mountain ridge which lay between Jerusalem on the north and the scene of their former wilderness life on the south. Ephraim, Manasseh, and one or two smaller tribes obtained the more fruitful hill country to the north of Jerusalem and south of the plains of Esdraelon and Jezreel, which cut across the mountain ridge of Canaan from the Mediterranean to the Jordan just south of the Sea of Galilee.

In the hills of Galilee, to the north of Esdraelon, another group of tribes found a foothold, though intermingling greatly with the former inhabitants.

The Canaanites still held the fruitful plain which separated the two northern groups of tribes, and also the stronghold of Jerusalem with a line of towns, reaching down to the Mediterranean plain, that cut Judah off from her northern kinsmen. To the west of Judah, on the coast plain, lay the group of allied city-states of the Philistines, a people who had entered Canaan from the northwest at about the time of Israel's entrance from the east.

In this era Egypt, torn with internal dissensions, had ceased to exercise any control over Canaan, and the Israelites, Philistines, and older inhabitants were left to contend with one another for control. It is not possible to trace the order of events for the next century, but the older sources make it clear that Israel's final predominance was won in part by alliance and absorption of the Canaanites, in part by desperate struggle.

d) The united kingdom (ca. 1040–940 B.C.).— War with the Philistines was the immediate occasion of the uniting of all the tribes under the first king, Saul. David's successful completion of this series of contests, with his conquests of Ammon, Edom, Moab, and his alliances with Phoenicia and other neighbors, gave Israel real national unity and complete dominance for the time. Jerusalem, which David captured and made his capital, was most favorably situated, lying as it did between the northern and the southern tribes. Solomon retained through his long reign most of the territory which his father had won, and he engaged in foreign trade on a scale that gave the capital much magnificence for so small a state.

e) *The divided kingdom* (*ca. 940–722 and 586 B.C.*).—The liberty-loving tribes of the north, objecting to the despotic rule and severe taxation of the Judean Solomon, revolted after the king's death. They accepted one of their own number, Jeroboam, as their ruler and left to Solomon's son Rehoboam only Judah and the tiny tribe of Benjamin, whose territory lay close to Jerusalem. Depleted Simeon, which had met severe calamity in the period of conquest, had now disappeared as a separate tribal unit.

The relatively strong Northern Kingdom now waged a life-and-death struggle with the Aramean or Syrian power, whose center was at Damascus. Sometimes it was in alliance with Judah, sometimes hostile to it. At length, after two centuries, the more distant and formidable kingdom of Assyria deported a portion of the Israelites, settled pagan peoples conquered elsewhere among the remnant, and made the mixed population thus formed an integral part of the Assyrian Empire.

Judah, in a more sheltered position, continued to abide in the land, sometimes independent, sometimes tributary to Assyria, Egypt, or Babylonia, until revolt against her Babylonian overlord, Nebuchadrezzar, led to her destruction in 586 B.C. with the deportation of many thousands of her inhabitants to Babylonia.

f) The exile (586–538 B.C.).—After 586 B.C. some 50,000 of the best elements of the Jews were living in Babylonia, and many others were voluntary exiles in Egypt, whither they had fled. In Palestine the peasantry still remained on the Judean hills as a distant and insignificant part of Nebuchadrezzar's great kingdom. In the course of a few years some of those who had fled to Egypt returned, but otherwise conditions continued largely unchanged until Cyrus the Persian conquered Babylon in 538 B.C.

g) The Persian age (538–332 B.C.).—Cyrus marks a new era in human history with his policy of respecting the racial and national traits of the peoples who made up his great empire. Under him, and later under Darius, who organized the empire, the Jews were permitted to rebuild Jerusalem and the temple and to enjoy the local rule of a descendant of the line of David as governor of the sub-province of Judea.

The greater part of the Jews preferred to remain in Babylonia, where they had now become established in the business life of that commercial district; it was chiefly "the people of the land," those left behind, who rebuilt the city and the temple.

At length, about a century after Cyrus' conquest, an eastern Jew, Nehemiah, who had risen to a position of trust in the Persian court, was appointed governor of Judea with authority to rebuild the walls of Jerusalem and make the city defensible. The carrying out of his mission made possible the separation of Jewish life and worship from that of the neighboring peoples, especially the half-pagan Samaritans. These were the mixed descendants of the old northern Israelites and the peoples whom the Assyrians had forcibly settled among them three centuries before.

h) *The Greek age (332–168 B.C.).*—When, in 332 B.C., Alexander of Macedon marched from his conquest of Phoenicia to Egypt, Judea fell under Greek rule and, after Alexander's death, became a bone of contention between the Egyptian and Syrian divisions of his empire. For more than a century it remained much of the time under the Ptolemies of Egypt, and then, for a generation, continuously under the Seleucids of Syria, until the mad attempt of the king, Antiochus Epiphanes, to force complete Hellenization upon the Jews led to desperate revolt.

i) *The Maccabean era (168–63 B.C.).*—The uprising against Syria was led by an aged priest who was soon succeeded by his son, Judas Maccabeus. Judas, by a series of brilliant victories, gained control of Jerusalem and re-established there the Jewish worship which Antiochus had stopped. After the death of Judas in battle, his brothers carried on the struggle and ultimately gained full independence from Syria, a position retained by their descendants until the eastward advance of Rome brought Pompey to Damascus and thence to Jerusalem. During their rule the Maccabees extended their territory to include essentially the area of the old united kingdom of David and Solomon.

j) The Roman age (63 B.C.–70 A.D., 135 A.D., and beyond).—The year 63 B.C. marks the beginning of Rome's control over Palestine. Pompey, whose aid was sought by rival claimants for the Jerusalem throne, brought the country under Roman supervision almost without a struggle.

In the troubled days of the overthrow of the Roman Republic and the strifes that followed, Palestine experienced many vicissitudes before it came under the rule of Herod as a *rex socius* of Rome. This Herod was a descendant of the ancient Edomites, who had been forcibly incorporated into Judaism by one of the Maccabean rulers.

With the death of Herod in 4 B.C. his kingdom was divided among three of his sons, who were allowed only the minor title of tetrarch. The failure of the oldest to rule Judea successfully led to the sending of a Roman procurator in 6 A.D.

Sixty years later the corruption of the proc-
urators and their inability to understand the
Jewish temper led to the outbreak of a four
years' war that ended with the destruction of
Jerusalem in the year 70 A.D. The temple worship ceased from that day, but the other observ-
ances of the Jewish religion continued in other
parts of the land.

Many rabbis established themselves as a religious college and court at Jamnia on the coast
plain, and there that discussion and application of
the Law which later developed into that great
body of authoritative Jewish writings known as
the Talmud was continued. Throughout the land,
too, the synagogues, which had become the great
force for popular religious instruction, continued
for centuries to shape the life and thought of
children and adults alike.

In 132 A.D. desperate revolt inspired by messianic
hopes broke out. After three years of frightful car-
nage and devastation, Israel's struggles for political independence ceased. The impressive ruins of
synagogues in Galilee, dating from the second and
third centuries A.D., indicate that even the last war
for independence could not destroy the Hebrew
religion in the land. Many generations earlier,
however, the Jews had carried their synagogue and
their ancient writings with them throughout the
civilized world; the future of Judaism had come to

rest with the Dispersion and so to be independent of the outward changes in Palestine or any other one land.

SUPPLEMENTARY READING

Marti, *Religion of the Old Testament*, pp. 1–71.
Paton, *The Early Religion of Israel*, pp. 1–34.
Addis, *Hebrew Religion*, pp. 1–52.
Ottley, *The Religion of Israel*, pp. 1–24.
Peters, *The Religion of the Hebrews*, pp. 61–80.
H. P. Smith, *The Religion of Israel*, pp. 12–45.
J. M. P. Smith, *The Prophet and His Problems*, pp. 3–35.

CHAPTER II

THE DELIVERANCE AND THE COVENANT

References for study—

   (1) Amos 2:10; 3:1–2; Hos. 2:14–23; 11:1–4;
   12:13; 13:4–8; Jer. 2:2; Mic. 6:4.
   (2) Exod. 3:2–4a, c, 5, 7, 8a, 16, 17a, 18; 3:1, 4b, d,
   6, 9–15; 6:2–8.
   (3) Amos 8:5.
   (4) Judg. 5:4–5; I Kings 19:1–14; Exod. 19:2–25.
   (5) Exod. 33:5–11, chaps. 25–27; Num., chap. 2.

Note in group (1) the significance of the deliverance
and wilderness period in the teaching of the prophets; in
(2) the points of agreement and difference in the threefold
account of the revelation to Moses at the bush; in (3) the
connection between new moon and Sabbath; in (4) the
connection of Yahweh with Sinai-Horeb; in (5) the early
account of the tent of meeting and the late priestly account
of the tabernacle and its furniture and the arrangement of
the camp.

The deliverance from Egypt and the events
following in the wilderness marked for the Hebrews
the beginning of their national religion. The
national historians differed as to whether their
ancestors had known God as Yahweh before
their sojourn in Egypt, but they agreed that he
became their national God and they his people
by the deliverance and the covenant at his sacred

23

mountain. To the prophet Amos this was the proof that Yahweh had known Israel alone of all the families of the earth; to Hosea it was the father's care for a tenderly loved child. These and other prophets pointed back to the wilderness as the place where Israel was won a pure bride and where her religious practices were simple and uncorrupted.

The national historians, writing centuries later than the events, ascribed to this period a formulation of laws and an organization of worship that is quite out of harmony with the prophets' direct appeals to the consciousness of the nation and with the subsequent history as indicated in the earliest sources.

To determine with certainty just which elements of the Hebrew religious belief and practice date from the wilderness period and which are of later origin is impossible with present knowledge; yet most recent writers agree that a source of the differences which mark off the religion of Israel from all others is to be found in the experience of the deliverance from Egypt and the covenant at the mountain.

Budde emphasizes the covenant, a contract voluntarily made, as the basis for the moral appeal in the religion. When a god is thought of as belonging always to a tribe or people, as, for example, Asshur, god of Assyria, Marduk, god of Babylon, Chemosh, god of Moab, the deity cannot cast off his people if they are unfaithful to him. He may show his anger by permitting them to suffer defeats and losses, but in the end his glory and theirs are indissolubly united; their destruction might leave him without any to pay him honor, and might even obliterate his name from the earth. In the case of Israel and Yahweh there was no such inherent connection. He had voluntarily chosen them when he existed apart from and independent of them, and they had voluntarily accepted him as their God. It was a marriage, a contract, a covenant. Now if either party breaks a contract the other is free.

Paton emphasizes the threefold account of Yahweh's appearance to Moses when tending the flock of his father-in-law as agreeing in the central point of the revelation of Yahweh's determination to deliver Israel from Egypt and to give her the land of Caanan. He finds in this two new and vital points: the first of these is the fact that a deity upon whom the people had no vital claim had compassion upon them when they were oppressed. This, he says, "was a new sort of divinity in the Semitic world"; "he was a god with a moral character who transcended the ancient limitations of tribal religion." The second point is that the deliverance shows this deity more powerful than other gods—no local baal limited in action to one district. "In these two new ideas that were destined to work a revolution in the history of religion," he adds, "we cannot fail to recognize a genuine revelation of God to Moses."

Whether Israel's ancestors had previously known their God as Yahweh or not, the coming of the conception of God's character and nature as of one willing and able to deliver the oppressed tribes from mighty Egypt may well be counted the true birthday of the Hebrew faith. The nation's later religious teachers made no error in laying the stress they did upon the exodus.

Montefiore, following Wellhausen in part, makes prominent the establishing of the sanctuary at Kadesh and the giving of decisions there upon matters brought for settlement; he infers that Moses thus taught social morality as a part of Yahweh's religion, and he finds that the Mosaic religion contained the conception that Yahweh was just, as well as powerful, that he alone was to be worshiped by all the tribes of Israel and would not only lead them to victory, but, through his interpreters, would become Israel's lawgiver and judge.

We may find truth in each of these views; a combination of their truths will probably give us a more adequate conception of the real significance of Moses and of his period than any one of them alone.

The contract or covenant idea of Israel's relation to her God gives her religious teachers in subse-

quent centuries ground for most effective demand
for an exclusive devotion to the national God, a
demand which appeals to some of the best elements
of man's moral nature. The thought of this God
as not belonging by nature to Israel proves a basis
also for ultimate monotheism. Of itself, however,
this one source affords no complete and adequate
explanation.

Emphasis upon the compassion of Yahweh in
the deliverance from Egypt is equally justified by
the teaching of Israel's prophets and equally vital
in any satisfactory explanation of the origin of the
Hebrew religion. Again, there is ground for stress-
ing the significance of Moses' work in establishing
justice among men as the representative of God.
We may recognize that the holding of a tribunal
at a shrine, in the name of a god, was familiar to
the nomad Arabs generally and that Moses' activity
in this respect was no new and distinctive feature
in the Yahweh religion; yet we may well believe
that the priestly function of Moses in giving judicial
decisions at the sanctuary served to supplement
his prophetic teaching of God's compassionate
choice and the influence of the covenant idea as
one of the sources of Israel's later religion.

We must draw our conclusions as to the character of the social morality fostered by the work
of Moses from later indications, since we cannot
with certainty trace individual laws back to his

time. It is true that Peters, in his recent *Religion of the Hebrews*, ably defends the Mosaic authority of the essence of the Ten Commandments found in Exod. 20:1–17 and Deut. 5:6–21, but most scholars are convinced that even this brief code contains elements that belong to a later era of social development.

The exact era when particular laws were first enunciated in Israel is a matter of quite secondary importance in comparison with the fundamental questions which we have been considering. The discovery of the law code of King Hammurabi, who ruled Babylon centuries before the time of Moses, has shown that the laws of the Pentateuch would hardly be Moses' most distinctive contribution, even if they had all been formulated by him. In some cases the close parallelism between these older Babylonian laws and those of Israel shows that at some stage the Hebrews received from the Canaanites or other Semites ideas of legal justice that were far more ancient than the age of Moses. In other instances Israel's code even represented a less highly developed stage of social justice than that of ancient Babylonia. In the matter of mitigating the cruelty of penalties, however, the Hebrew laws show an advance upon those of Hammurabi.

In the present study the great law codes will be considered in the era when they were certainly already formulated and made known to the people. In connection with the era of Moses we limit our consideration to the ethical spirit lying at the roots of Israel's later legal system. Peters notes that the moral commands of the Decalogue, the sixth to the tenth, can all be paralleled in the famous confession of the Egyptian religion by which the soul of the dead was to vindicate himself before Osiris, averring that he had not stolen, murdered, etc. He thinks that Moses may have derived a suggestion of a sacred law from Egypt. The view that intercourse with the Egyptians might be the source of Moses' ideas of morality was already advocated many years ago, and more recent study of the ethical side of Egyptian religion tends to strengthen the inference.

Hundreds of years before the exodus, at about the time of Hammurabi, when social justice had been embodied in so excellent a law code in Babylon, social prophets had appeared in Egypt and social justice had even become the official doctrine of the state. In Ikhnaton's brief monotheistic reform a few centuries later "truth" and "justice" appear as prominent ideals. Although Egypt had already returned to her old gods several generations before the Hebrew exodus, the ideal of god as a "just judge not accepting a bribe, uplifting the insignificant, [protecting] the poor," was one that animated the prayers of the poor in Egypt at the

time of the Hebrew oppression and deliverance.
We may reasonably infer that some Egyptian
ethical influence was united with the experiences
of the wilderness, where Yahweh was thought to
dwell upon the cloud-enshrouded summit of his
sacred mountain, in the preparation of Moses for
the revelation which he received at the flaming
bush, and that this helped to fit him for his administration of justice at the Kadesh sanctuary. This
administration, as we have noted, helped to fix
at the very roots of the Hebrew religion the idea
of Yahweh as one who cared for human rights.

Of religious institutions, practices, and objects,
we have noted in the previous chapter that simple
sacrifices, the rite of circumcision, and the tendency
to associate mountains, springs, stones, and trees
with the divine presence and revelation to man,
were a part of the people's racial heritage.

The simple spring festival of the Passover, with
its lamb consumed between evening and morning,
is to be recognized as a part of the ritual that dates
back to the life of the wilderness. It resembles
closely the sacramental meal of Arabian paganism
in its general form and in some details and well
illustrates that primitive form of Semitic sacrifice
where nothing is offered as tribute to the god, but
where he shares the communal meal with his people.
The original character of the ceremony is accord-
ingly preserved in the Lord's Supper of Christian-

ity, although modified in form; it is a "sacrament" and a "communion."

Other of Israel's annual feasts show by their character or history that they are of later origin. Feasts of harvest and vintage, for example, find place only in agricultural life. The Sabbath, too, as a day of cessation from regular labor is an institution which the nature of nomad life renders impracticable. Hebrew literature connects the Sabbath with the new moon, and Babylonian writings show that the times of the moon's changes had a certain significance as days when some sorts of activity were taboo, much as in the case of Friday among the superstitious today. That the Hebrew Sabbath was connected with the phases of the moon in its origin seems clear, and it may have been a modified form of the Babylonian *shabattum*, or time of the moon's change. Babylonian ideas had a far more direct opportunity to influence Israel after the settlement in Canaan than during the wilderness period; hence this line of consideration also favors the probability that it was after the period considered in the present chapter that the institution of the Sabbath appeared in Israel. In any case its distinctive significance in the Jewish religion is hardly to be traced to the Mosaic era.

Of religious places and objects the mountain of Yahweh, known to different Hebrew writers as

Sinai and Horeb, is first to be noted.   Here Moses had his vision at the bush, and hither he led his people to meet with the God who had wrought their deliverance from Egypt.   Christian tradition has placed the mountain in the little peninsula between the two arms of the Red Sea, but a careful study of all the Biblical data makes it more probable that it was one of the volcanic peaks south of the Dead Sea, and hence nearer to the fountain of Kadesh, which would lie to the westward of the mountain.   Here some of the awe-inspiring aspects of nature must have united with the memory of recent experiences in Egypt and at the Red Sea to impress the people with the majesty and power of the God who made his especial abode upon this mountain summit and yet had been able to bring calamities to the Egyptians, distant many days' journey across the desert.   While their God's power must have been thus recognized from the outset as not limited to the one district, here was his peculiar abode where he especially revealed himself to his chosen interpreter.

After the people had crossed the Jordan, their poets still for long delighted to picture Yahweh as coming in the majesty of cloud, lightning, and thunder from his storm-wreathed mountain seat to the deliverance of his people.   Centuries after the settlement in Canaan, in his loneliness and despair, the true prophet of Yahweh, Elijah, journeyed to

Horeb for a new vision of the God who had at first revealed himself there.

For the mass of the people to conceive their God as going with them and taking up his abode in Canaan where other lords were already established as firmly as Yahweh on Sinai-Horeb was exceedingly difficult. The portable ark and the tent of meeting which sheltered it helped to impress upon the people that Yahweh's presence accompanied them wherever they journeyed and encamped. The old song for the taking up and setting down of the ark is counted one of the earliest literary fragments of Israel and very probably dates from the period of the wilderness:

> Rise up, O Yahweh,
> And make thine enemies to flee,
> And let them fly who hate thee.
>
> Return, O Yahweh,
> And bless the myriads
> Of Israel's clans.

At any rate the ark of Yahweh's presence seems clearly to come from the Mosaic time. Here again there is the possibility of suggestion from a somewhat similar object in Egyptian religious symbolism.

The contents of the ark have been the object of much speculation in recent years. If the Decalogue in any form dates back to the Mosaic era, we may accept the later tradition that it was

inscribed upon stone tablets placed in the ark.
It has been recently argued in favor of the Mosaic
character of the "Ten Words" that there was no
favorable opportunity for the replacing of any
earlier contents of the ark by such tables between
the time of Moses and the time of written reference
to the tables in the ark.   Others surmise that the
chest originally contained some uninscribed sacred
stone or stones, a beth-el—an earlier relic which
Moses adopted as a symbol somewhat as Mahomet,
despite his lofty doctrine of the spiritual Deity,
still retained the Kaaba or sacred stone of Mecca.
All this is uncertain inference; the ark itself and
the tent of meeting are all of which we can feel at
all sure as symbols of God's presence when Israel
moved away from the sacred mountain.

Late priestly tradition constructed in imagination an elaborate portable sanctuary, the tabernacle, after the model of Solomon's temple, and
arranged the wilderness camp symmetrically with
this as the center.   The earlier history knows only
a tent of meeting, pitched without the camp,
whither individuals went to consult God and
where Moses went to speak with him face to face.

The stay at Sinai was comparatively brief; the
spring of Kadesh, whose name "Sacred" or
"Sanctuary" suggests the ancient character of the
place as one of the sacred springs of which mention
has been made, formed the center of Israel's life

during the major part of the wilderness period.
Here, as we have seen, Moses laid the foundation
of Israel's social morality as he dispensed justice
in the name of Yahweh.

While critical study of the sources of Hebrew
history follows the earlier prophets of the nation
in denying to the Mosaic age the elaborate theo-
cratic organization of society and worship ascribed
to it in later tradition, the true sources of the
highest development of Hebrew religion are to be
found in the work of Moses. In the name of the
God of power and compassion he led the tribes out
of bondage to freedom, brought them into voluntary covenant relation with this God, established
his worship with the simple forms congenial to a
life of nomad character, taught the people that this
God was not limited in his presence to one sacred
spot, and for many years administered justice as
the agent of the Deity.

SUPPLEMENTARY READING

Budde, *Religion of Israel to the Exile*, pp. 1–38.
Paton, *The Early Religion of Israel*, pp. 36–54.
Peters, *The Religion of the Hebrews*, pp. 81–110.
Addis, *Hebrew Religion*, pp. 53–77.
Ottley, *The Religion of Israel*, pp. 25–40.
Peake, *The Religion of Israel*, pp. 1–26.
H. P. Smith, *The Religion of Israel*, pp. 46–62.
Montefiore, *Origin and Growth of Religion as Illustrated by the Religion of the Ancient Hebrews*, pp. 32–54.

CHAPTER III

THE WARS OF YAHWEH

References for study—

  (1) Gen. 22:1–19; Exod. 22:29; I Kings 16:34; II
      Kings 3:26–27; 16:3; 21:6; Mic. 6:7; Jer. 7:31.
  (2) Hos. 2:8.
  (3) Josh. 13:13; 17:12, 13; Judg. 1:19–21, 27–36;
      3:5a, 6.
  (4) Judg., chaps. 17, 18; I Sam. 9:11–25; I Kings
      18:30–33; I Sam. 19:13–16.
  (5) I Sam. 4:1–11; 6:1—7:2.
  (6) Judg., chap. 5.
  (7) I Sam. 9:1—10:14; 19:18–24; II Kings 3:13–15.

Note in (1) the familiarity of Israel with idea of child sacrifice; in (2) the failure of Israel to understand that Yahweh gave fruits of soil; in (3) the real character of the conquest; in (4) the images and practices of worship; in (5) the fate of the ark; in (6) how fully tribes united in great struggle and the spirit that roused them; in (7) the work of Samuel and practices of other early prophets.

Intermingling of the tent-dwelling Bedawin and the village-dwelling agriculturalists is a constant phenomenon in Canaan. The traveler meets occasional Bedawins in and about Jerusalem itself, and six or eight miles away on the borders of the wilderness of Judea he may chance upon a considerable encampment of their black goats'-

36

hair tents. East of the Jordan nomad camps and
stone-built towns, with their surrounding grain
fields, are closely associated. Sometimes the
settled inhabitants in these regions are forced to
evacuate their villages and seek other homes when
the Bedawin raids upon their fields and stock
become unendurable. The true nomad prefers
his bed in the open tent to any closer shelter, but
the fruits of settled agricultural life also attract
him irresistibly. When a season of drought
makes his usual pasture lands unequal to the support
of his flocks, his pressure upon the more settled
districts becomes especially severe.

Nomad life from before the dawn of history
down to the present day has of necessity been
essentially the same, even in its details. The constant ebb and flow of its tide, too, against the
borders and far up into the inlets between the
towns and cultivated fields of Canaan is ever
the same. About the year 1400 B.C. the governor
of Jerusalem wrote to his king, the Pharaoh of
Egypt: "The king has no longer any territory,
the Habiri have devastated all the king's territory.
If troops come this year, the territory will remain
my lord, the king's, but if no troops come the
territory of my lord, the king, is lost." Three
hundred years later, when Israel had found settlement in the land, "because of Midian the children
of Israel made them the dens which are in the

mountains, and the caves, and the strongholds. And so it was when Israel had sown, that the Midianites came up, and the Amalekites, and the children of the east; they came up against them; and they encamped against them, and destroyed the increase of the earth, till thou come unto Gaza, and left no sustenance in Israel, neither sheep, nor ox, nor ass. For they came up with their cattle and their tents; they came in as locusts for multitude; both they and their camels were without number; and they came into the land to destroy it."

So it has been from time immemorial to the present; sometimes it is a night's raid that sweeps back before the dawn; sometimes it is a coming with flocks and tents and a more or less permanent settlement in the land. Despite the persistence of nomad life in Arabia and about its borders, there is always a passing over, near the borders, from pastoral to agricultural life, from the tent village to the stone village. The town-dwellers are fain often to make the best terms they can with their new and undesired neighbors.

Thus it is possible to observe to some extent, even today, the kind of social changes that Israel experienced when she moved from Kadesh to the plateaus and slopes east of the Jordan valley, and then across the Jordan into Canaan. At first she was able to capture but few walled towns and settled chiefly in the open country. Here, pre-

sumably, her tents often continued to be her dwell-
ings. Only after several generations, partly by
capture, more often by peaceful penetration and
covenant with the earlier inhabitants, did she
really come to possess and dominate the land.
In this process it was necessary to learn the culture
of the soil and all the arts of settled life from those
who were ultimately subdued and absorbed.

Among the Canaanites the proper propitiation
of the local baals who controlled the fruitfulness
of the soil was an important part of the art of agriculture. In accepting Yahweh at Sinai as the
covenant God of all the associated tribes Israel
had by no means reached the point of denying
the existence of other deities. In Canaan crop
troubles would be frequent enough to prove that
the Hebrew farmer who did not fully recognize by
the appropriate rites the long-established baals of
the land was reaping only the consequences of his
impiety. It may be true, as has been suggested,
that anyone who withheld the customary sacrifice
would be forced by the majority to perform it or
to leave the community to prevent him from bringing misfortune upon his neighbors.

It was doubtless during this period of transition
that Israel adopted the observance of the harvest
and vintage festivals which later formed a prominent part of her worship of Yahweh, much as
Christianity spreading in pagan Europe adopted

the practices of old heathen festivals and turned them into Christian memorial days. Long centuries passed before Israel as a whole came to ascribe the fertility-giving functions of the local baals to the God of Sinai. In part the people worshiped the baals, in part Yahweh, and sometimes they did not discriminate much between the two.

Worship of the lords of fertility involved in vine-growing Canaan, as in the Dionysiac festivals of the Greeks, wild excess of wine and all that went with it. In the Canaanite religion the Ashteroth, goddesses of fertility, were worshiped no less than the Baalim. Chastity was sacrificed in their honor and sacred harlots were connected with the sanctuaries. Still further, the offspring granted by the deities must be sanctified by offering the first-born. Not only were the offspring of flocks and herds thus devoted, but child sacrifice was a regular Canaanite practice. The excavations at the old Canaanite city of Gezer, for example, have given gruesome evidence of this, and many passages in the Old Testament show how familiar the Hebrews were with the practice and how at times they adopted it, although their religious leaders strongly opposed it.

Both economic considerations—the effort to secure by divine favor good crops, multiplying flocks, and abundant offspring—and the gratification of bodily appetites united to draw the

Hebrews to the worship of the Baalim and Ashteroth of Canaan, even though they might continue
to recognize Yahweh as the great god who had
delivered them from Egypt, and had cared for them
in the wilderness. Four centuries after the entrance into Canaan the prophet Hosea was bitterly
denouncing Israel for supposing that it was Baal
and not Yahweh who gave the grain, new wine,
and oil.

In looking back we may see that the adoption
of Canaanite worship with its gross excesses was
humanly inevitable in the transition from the
simple austere life of the wilderness to the relatively complex and luxurious life of Canaan. The
ability to accept the good and reject all the evil
from a higher stage of material civilization is never
widely prevalent in an age of transition. To some
strict religionists, as we noted in the first chapter,
the only course open was to reject all the distinctive practices of Canaan as evil.

The old narrative of Micah's sanctuary and the
migration of the Danites, preserved as an appendix
to the Book of Judges, throws much light on the
primitive conditions of Yahweh-worship in the
early days of Israel in Canaan. We find that an
image is desirable and no object of offense as connected with this worship, and that a sanctuary
may be set up by any individual or tribe. To
officiate at such a sanctuary a member of the tribe

of Levi is desirable, but does not seem to be counted necessary.   There is no indication in the story that any of these features gives offense to the narrator or participants, although they are directly opposed to those Old Testament laws which prohibit images, limit the sanctuary to Jerusalem, and strictly confine the priesthood to one family group out of the tribe of Levi.   It seems clear that such laws were unknown at the time of this narrative.

Subsequent records indicate that ideas similar to those of the old story as to images, place of worship, and priestly functions persisted for generations after Dan's conquest of Laish, even among the best and leading men of the nation, such as Samuel, David, Elijah.   The development of the stricter rules of worship will be considered in later chapters.

At Shiloh, in the tribe of Ephraim, the tent of meeting was pitched, or some more permanent and elaborate structure raised, to shelter the ark. Here the sacred symbol of God's presence rested for many years, except when it was taken forth as a palladium into battle in time of direst need. After the capture of the ark by the Philistines and its singular return, it remained long in comparative neglect until David's time.

A survey of the era of the conquest shows that, from certain points of view, there was a retrogression from the Mosaic age.   The separation of

the tribes into three or four groups not only forced
each group to make good its position in the land
with comparatively little help from the others,
but tended to weaken loyalty to the God of the
confederation, who, even in Moses' lifetime,
had probably not drawn away the loyalty of
the people wholly from old family and tribal
deities.

Once during the century between Moses and
Samuel we have record of a considerable number
of the tribes acting together. This was in the
great battle on the plain of Esdraelon, described
in the contemporary "Song of Deborah." Even
on this occasion nearly as many tribes are condemned for failing to come to the battle as are
praised for participating, and some are unmentioned, as though their co-operation was not to be
expected. Judah, it would seem, was too fully
separated from all the tribes of the north to be
thought of as sharing in their struggles. Amid all
this separation and consequent weakness the fact
stands out clearly in the old victory ode that "To
the help of Yahweh" was the cry that could rouse
the tribes to any sort of united effort. This fact
was significant with promise for the next stage of
the people's development.

Even in the first century of transition to settled
agricultural life we may recognize the preparation
of the people for real religious advance. We have

seen the transition fraught with the gravest dangers that the Canaanite life would efface or change beyond recognition the faith that had made a promising beginning at Sinai and Kadesh, and we must recognize that the Canaanite religion brought in elements of worship which continued to be a grave detriment to Israel's religion; yet there was a genuine enrichment of the Mosaic religion from the elements absorbed. This enrichment consisted in part in recognition of human dependence upon divine power in all the new and varied experiences of daily life in agriculture and town affairs. Life was religious among the Canaanites; their places of worship were everywhere in the land. More than a hundred sanctuaries are mentioned, Paton states, in the older writings of the Old Testament, most of which can be shown to have been primitive shri of the land of Canaan.

Ultimately Yahweh displaced the Canaanite deities at these shrines, and thus the people came slowly to think of him and to worship him in connection with the personal and local affairs of their daily life. It was impossible for the mass of the people even to come to know the great and awful Deity of Sinai's thunder clouds, the God of all Israel, as concerned in their ordinary life and industry, except by the road they traveled of first mingling with his worship that of the agricultural Canaanites.

The Israel of the time of the conquest was a primitive people without much capacity for large generalizations. Even today the more primitive adherents of the great monotheistic religions of Mohammedanism and Christianity find their religious faith quickened at the local shrines of the saints who touch their consciousness more closely than a universal God.

The forms of worship adopted were demoralizing in the extreme, and yet, after the long struggle of Yahweh and the Baalim, much of the Canaanite ritual was preserved in purified form in the religion of Israel, and its ceremonies became a mighty force; they played a great part in preserving, through darkest days, faith in a God not made with hands, eternal in the heavens.

When Israel had largely made good her position among the earlier inhabitants of Canaan, she was threatened with absorption by the strong coalition of the Philistine city-states that had recently been formed on the coast plain. At this juncture there appeared the most significant figure that had arisen since Moses' death, a century or more before, the seer or prophet Samuel. More or less in association with Samuel there appeared also companies of religious enthusiasts, known as "sons of the prophets," moving about the land with music and song. These figures were symptomatic of a larger religio-patriotic spirit springing up among the people.

Samuel realized the work that must be done, and he recognized in the unawakened giant, Saul, the man through whom the new enthusiasm might be united in effective action. He succeeded in bringing Saul under the contagious enthusiasm of one of the companies of prophets and left him to find his opportunity for action. The time was ripe, and the occasion soon came which made Saul the permanent leader of a far greater coalition of the tribes than that of Deborah's time.

Again, loyalty to the covenant God of Israel played a large part in making possible united action by the tribes. Since this united action resulted in the establishment of the monarchy, and ultimately in complete political supremacy in Canaan, the nation may justly be said to have been born from the religion of Yahweh. The successful founding of the kingdom made it clear to all that the God who had once delivered from Egypt now ruled in Canaan.

The struggles of Israel that marked the century and a half between the departure from Kadesh and the firm establishment of the monarchy tended, no doubt, to emphasize one side of God's nature at the expense of other aspects. We may see in our own day the outbreak of a great war producing a revival of religious faith and worship, affecting many who have been absorbed in industrial activities or pleasures; but the type of religion

is exceedingly one-sided. The Lord worshiped
is a God of war, invoked, it may be, as a national
God, or at best as arbiter among the struggling
nations, hardly as the compassionate father of all.
Since this is so, we can understand how Yahweh
must have appeared chiefly as God of hosts in the
days of the life-and-death struggle between the
times of Moses and of David.

A poetic fragment quoted in the Book of Numbers is ascribed to the Book of the Wars of Yahweh.
This lost book, whose name we know only from
this incidental reference, was presumably made up
of songs growing up in connection with the struggle
for Canaan, and may well have contained many
odes similar to the Deborah song, and ascribing
Israel's victories to the aid of her God.

The stress laid by this age on Yahweh as the
God of battles is no direct advance in ideal upon
the Mosaic time, yet it was by such rude and narrow paths that the people came to general recognition of the God of Sinai as one able and willing to
care for them in the land of Canaan. This recognition was really a very great advance, for on the
intellectual side of religion there was perhaps no
more difficult step for an ancient Semitic people
to take than to dissociate a god permanently from
his traditional home. Such dissociation, however,
was a necessary advance if monotheism was to be
attained.

With the appearance of Samuel and the companies of prophets near the close of this era we take up the history of that phase of Israel's religion which was destined to be the great factor in its higher and universal development. Like nearly all origins, the source of prophecy is obscure. In the narrative concerning Samuel and Saul the statement occurs that he who is now called a prophet was aforetime called a *roeh*, "seer," and the story indicates that seers were looked upon as a sort of diviners, accustomed for a piece of silver to give aid in finding lost objects or in case of any similar need.

Samuel becomes distinguished in the story from seers of this kind and proves worthy of the title prophet in its late Hebrew sense as a spokesman of God, devoted to the best interests of his people and enlightened to direct their history into new channels. At the same time he is practically priest, officiating at the local sanctuary. In his day priest and seer had not yet been fully distinguished. The chief function of each was to ascertain the divine will and purpose. So far as there was distinction, it was probably chiefly in the means of ascertaining the hidden future. The priest would gain his knowledge by casting the sacred lot or by observing the organs of the sacrificial victims, while the seer would cultivate ecstacy and trance.

The companies of prophets, through whom
Samuel works in part, have not appeared in the
traditions of earlier times, but henceforth are met
occasionally in the history. Samuel is not one of
these, and in his action and speech he exhibits
nothing of the extravagant emotion characteristic
of the early members of the prophetic order. He
resembles much more closely Moses, whom the
later writers style a prophet, or Isaiah, who did
his work three centuries later.

Some have thought of the companies of prophets
as of Canaanitish origin, and this may be the case.
The word translated "prophet," *nabi*, quite probably refers by derivation to ecstasy, and the prophesying ascribed to the companies of Samuel's time
seems to have been of an ecstatic sort. In the old
story of the non-Israelite prophet, Balaam, unnat-
ural excitement seems to have been regarded as
the appropriate condition for oracular utterance.
Saul when he joins the company of prophets lies
all night stripped of his garment, and even as late
as Elisha a minstrel might be called on to induce
a trance condition in a prophet. The bands of
prophets that appear in Israel thus shared the
external characteristics of the prophets found
among other peoples.

In later Hebrew usage prophet meant a spokesman, one who uttered the message given to him
by God. In this sense Moses was more truly

a forerunner of the great prophets of Israel than the bands of prophets of Samuel's day. The greater prophets appear as lone figures, not as members of prophetic gilds, and they are notable among the great religious leaders of the world for their relative freedom from trance and ecstatic experience.

The age of transition from the wilderness to settled life was one necessarily of much confusion, marked by the loss of certain virtues and the adoption of many vices, and yet it is possible to trace, through all its obscurity, essential steps in the education of Israel toward the apprehension of the one God whose beneficent control shapes both the history of the nation and the daily life of man in his home and work.

SUPPLEMENTARY READING

Peake, *The Religion of Israel*, pp. 27–44.

Ottley, *The Religion of Israel*, pp. 41–60.

Marti, *Religion of the Old Testament*, pp. 72–116.

Paton, *The Early Religion of Israel*, pp. 55–115.

H. P. Smith, *The Religion of Israel*, pp. 63–82, 87–90, 117–30.

Budde, *Religion of Israel to the Exile*, pp. 39–104.

Peters, *The Religion of the Hebrews*, pp. 111–29, 170–73.

Addis, *Hebrew Religion*, pp. 78–134 (treats together the periods covered by this chapter and the next).

J. M. P. Smith, *The Prophet and His Problems*, pp. 36–58.

CHAPTER IV

RELIGION AND NATIONAL LIFE

References for study—

(1) I Sam. 26:17–19; II Sam. 21:1–14; 11:1—12:15.

(2) II Sam., chap. 6; I Kings, chap. 6; 11:1–8, 26–31; 12:25–30; II Kings 23:13–14.

(3) I Kings 5:13–16; 9:15–23, 26–29; 11:26–31.

(4) I Kings, chaps. 17–19, 21.

(5) Gen. 2:4a—4:15; 11:1–7; 12:1–4a, 6–8, 10–20; 13:2–11a; 18:1–8; 34:22–29; 39:2–9.

(6) Exod. 34:14a, 17, 18a, 19a, 20c, 21a, 22a, c, 25–28.

(7) Exod. 20:23–26; 22:20—23:19.

Note in (1) some aspects of morals and religion in David's time; in (2) the establishment of Yahweh-worship in Jerusalem, but recognition of other gods there; in (3) the economic conditions under Solomon and a prophet's attitude toward the kingdom; in (4) the real question at issue between Elijah and the reigning house; in (5) some religious and moral ideas and ideals in the Judean history; in (6) the character of the covenant code as given in the Judean history; in (7) places of worship, exclusiveness of Yahweh-worship, humanitarian provisions.

Saul's heroic struggle against the Philistines, despite early victories, ended in defeat and death. It remained for the next king, David, to become the successful founder of the Hebrew monarchy.

Later tradition made of David a man of lofty spiritual insight such as was actually attained in Israel only after long generations of development. David was a musician and poet, a general and states-man of no mean ability; he was also a loyal adher-ent of Yahweh, whose will he desired to execute, but in his understanding of that will he was a child of the era into which he was born, at the close of the days of the Judges.

One of the early narratives represents him as being told to go and serve other gods when he was driven across the border of Judea, since he would no longer be on Yahweh's territory. We have already noted that he had in his home a teraphim or household god, evidently an image which could be mistaken for David himself when it was covered in the bed. As king he permitted the savage blood-vengeance of the Gibeonites to fall upon seven of Saul's sons, whose dead bodies hung a grue-some sight from spring till autumn, in order to appease God's wrath and so relieve a famine that had oppressed the land.

Of David's outlaw life as chief of a band of free-booters, of his ruthless methods in warfare, and of his adultery with Bathsheba and his dastardly murder of her husband we need only remind our-selves in order to realize the primitive morals of this early hero. According to a portion of the narrative which many critics count a later tradition, David repented when the prophet Nathan led him to see the true nature of his sin. Even if the penitence be wholly historical, the narrative always puzzles those who are told that David was a man after God's own heart and who do not realize how crude was the apprehension of the divine will in David's age.

Despite the rudimentary character of morals and religion indicated by the early records of the times, the era was one of vital advancement for the religion of Israel. The political unification of all Canaan and the bringing of the ark to the newly won capital city meant a centralized recognition of Yahweh such as had not been known in the generations of struggle for the land. When the king brought the ark to Jerusalem, himself clad in a priest's garment, offering sacrifices and dancing or whirling like a dervish before the sacred symbol, he gave state recognition to the Yahweh religion such as had not been possible in the generations that preceded. Jerusalem was started then on the course of history that makes it today the most sacred spot in the world to loyal Jews and Christians alike, and second only to Mecca in the devotion of Mohammedans.

The fact that one who thus recognized Yahweh won victory for his people on all sides doubtless confirmed the faith of the mass of the Israelites that the wilderness God really ruled in Palestine, as nothing else could have done. David's victories with his public honoring of the God of Israel gave one of the greatest blows that the local gods of Canaan had received. The building of the temple by Solomon was a most impressive further step in the same direction. It is difficult to overestimate the wide influence of such visible marks of loyalty to the nation's God in the early days of national unity and strength.

We are not, however, to suppose that Solomon's temple at once became the one legitimate sanctuary in the land. Contemporary evidence shows clearly enough that the worship of Yahweh continued to be carried on at the old high places, and that it was characterized by the old debasing practices, so that to all outward appearances it differed but little from the worship of the Baalim and Ashteroth; nor was the one God the sole object of worship at Jerusalem itself.

The policy of foreign alliance sealed by royal marriages, that David had begun, was greatly developed by Solomon. This necessarily meant a recognition of foreign deities at the nation's capital; the marriage alliances would have proved a fruitful source of international discord if the princesses had been refused the right to worship their own deities. The high places that Solomon built for his foreign wives remained visible witnesses of the worship of other gods three centuries after he and the splendors of his court had passed.

Another aspect of Solomon's reign which tended to nullify the effect of the building of the temple is suggested by the statements in I Kings 6:38 and 7:1 that he was seven years in building the Lord's house and thirteen in building his own. The temple was in fact the royal chapel crowning a great collection of buildings whose extent and character placed a heavy drain upon the resources of a small and young kingdom. The northern tribes saw their labor expended year after year to beautify Jerusalem, which was far more closely identified with Judah than with their local interests and associations. The whole policy of Solomon, who sought to maintain his kingdom by establishing strongholds throughout the land and whose ambitions outstripped the resources of his state, meant for the people away from the immediate neighborhood of the capital loss of liberty, economic and political, such as they could not long endure.

Tradition, which represents David as listening to the guidance of priests interpreting the oracle and of prophets interpreting the moral character and will of God, is silent as to such guidance at Solomon's court; it pictures, rather, the prophetic influence which had formerly been active for national unity, now favoring division of the kingdom.

The separation that came shortly after Solomon's death left the temple as the sanctuary of the Southern and smaller Kingdom, made up of the two tribes that remained loyal to the house of Solomon and of their dependents. The Northern Kingdom adopted two old sanctuaries, about which many sacred traditions clustered, as its special seats of worship. The Jerusalem temple was much of a modern innovation connected with the hated taxation and despotism of Solomon's reign, and doubtless many of the forces of religious as well as political conservatism were with the Northern Kingdom. Even the golden calves may have found many defenders as the good old religious symbols under which God ought to be worshiped.

After some fifty years of vicissitude for Northern Israel, Omri came to the throne, a ruler who possessed something of the military and political ability of David. Entering into alliance with the old associate of David and Solomon, Phoenician Tyre, he married his son Ahab to Jezebel, the daughter of the Tyrian king. This masterful woman was not content merely to worship her father's god in her new home; she must needs propagate his faith there, so she introduced and made most popular among her husband's subjects the worship of the Tyrian Baal.

Phoenician religion was very similar to the old Canaanite worship, yet we should clearly dis-

tinguish the struggle with the Lord or Baal of
Tyre, which Jezebel introduced, in the ninth century,
from the earlier contest with the local baals of
Canaan. They had their prestige, as we saw,
through their long connection with the soil and
their supposed power to bless or curse the farmer
who tilled the land of their several districts. Baal
of Tyre came into the land under royal patronage
and as the mighty god of a great commercial city
whose ships sailed the distant seas and brought
back great treasure. In comparison with the
Phoenicians the people of Israel were poor and
provincial. Those who continued to worship only
Yahweh in the simple sanctuaries at Bethel and
Dan must have seemed very provincial to the
thousands who followed their queen in the cult of
her potent god in his temple at the new capital,
where Ahab had built his palace.

Jezebel's restless, ambitious spirit did not stop
with the introduction of a new fashion of worship.
She found her husband disposed to respect the
ancient rights of his subjects, however much he
might be vexed when one of them refused to
exchange or sell his ancestral vineyard which
the king wanted to add to his pleasure estate
in the fair valley of Jezreel. To the daughter of
the king of Tyre such a situation was simple of
solution; trump up a false charge against the
man, suborn some witnesses, secure conviction

and execution, and let the property revert to the crown.

At the crisis when a religion and its associated despotism, foreign to the people of Israel, threatened to establish all that they had revolted against when they split the kingdom, there appeared one of the most significant personalities in the history of Israel's religion. Many picturesque tales clustered about his memory and were treasured by his loyal followers, until at last a number of them found permanent preservation in our Books of Kings. Though the tales are early their character makes it difficult always to distinguish the actual course of events. Enough is clear, however, to make it evident that their hero, who bore the name "Yahweh is God" (Elijah), came from the region across the Jordan, where the ancient pastoral life of Israel had been more fully preserved than in Western Palestine, and that he dared face king and priests with a twofold demand: (1) that Yahweh alone should be recognized in Israel, and (2) that the ancient rights of the people should be respected even by the king.

It is worthy of note that it was on the occasion of Ahab's violation of a subject's right of property, rather than upon the direct issue of Baal-worship, that Elijah denounced in awful terms the coming overthrow of the dynasty. It is significant that the two demands in Yahweh's name were associated in the person and work of the one prophet, Elijah.

In an earlier chapter we have sought to find the roots of ancient Israel's belief in an ethical God, her faith that her God was himself righteous and required righteous dealings among men. We found in the Mosaic age various roots from which this faith may have sprung. In the years of struggle for the land and of the formation of the kingdom it is difficult to find evidence of advance in this direction. Indeed, as we have seen, the influences of Canaanite civilization and of the rude contests waged tended to make other aspects of religion dominant, yet there is adequate evidence that the Hebrew religion never lost its ethical tendency.

In the old oracular poem properly ascribed to the time of the united kingdom (Gen. 49:2-27) the fate of the tribes is interpreted as due to Yahweh's protecting care or to the violation of his righteous will. An act of lawlessness has cost Reuben his birthright, and the dividing and scattering of Simeon and Levi are due to their violence, probably their treachery in breaking covenant and slaying the Shechemites (Gen., chap. 34); Judah holds the royal scepter and Joseph enjoys the blessing of his father's God, who controls the sources of fruitfulness, which had formerly been under the power of the baals of the land.

The narrative of David's court and family life, now forming a considerable part of II Samuel and composed not long after the events narrated, reveals perhaps more clearly than the poem of Genesis, chapter 49, the ethical interpretation of religion—"the thing that David had done displeased Yahweh." "And Yahweh struck the child that Uriah's wife had borne unto David, and it was very sick." Even if we must drop out from between these two sentences the whole story of Nathan's rebuke and David's confession of sin, as reflecting the still higher ideals introduced by Hosea and Isaiah, the confessedly early narrative of David's family life still retains the consciousness that God cares for the maintenance of moral standards among men.

Elijah does not come as a preacher of ideals that are wholly new or have been wholly lost in the generations immediately preceding; yet he does stand forth in his great struggle against the rulers of his people as the forerunner of the great prophetic teachers who, a century later, carry his principles far beyond what he taught.

A historical study of the development of Israel's religion gives added meaning to the New Testament emphasis upon Elijah, with his simple message of righteousness, as the forerunner of the deeper and higher revelation that was to follow.

The rebellion of the greater part of the nation against the house of David was the assertion of human rights against extravagant and despotic monarchism. The united kingdom made possible freedom from foreign oppression; the division of the kingdom checked internal oppression. Both political changes are ascribed by Israel's historians to the influence of prophets. The spirit that makes human rights the end and holds government and rulers accountable to God for the realizing of this end is the true spirit of Hebrew prophecy, and this comes to dramatic expression in Naboth's vineyard. It was only on condition of learning the lessons which Elijah enforced that Israel could play an important part in the advancement of civilization.

It was not much later than the time of Elijah's work in the north that a writer, or group of writers, in the kingdom of Judah gathered together the old songs and tales of the people and arranged them in such a way as to tell a connected story from the creation of man, through the origin and development of the chosen people, to the organization of the kingdom. The dominant thought of the whole was Yahweh's continuous control in accordance with the principles of righteousness.

Religious motives made Israel a nation, and it was religious motives that led, two centuries later, to the attempt to tell the story of the nation's origin. The religious outlook attained by the Judean writers in the ninth century B.C. gave this first great attempt at writing connected history a scope that makes it one of the most important landmarks in the story of the world's literature. Four centuries later the Greeks would independently develop true historical literature; but the glory of first writing this had long since been acquired by the historiographers of Judah.

In the early Judean history a childlike tradition of the creation of life is made introductory to the great drama of human sin, suffering, and salvation. Man and woman created by Yahweh for pure fellowship with one another and with their Creator, through the desire of the eye and of the palate and the desire to know evil as well as good, defy their Creator's will and break the bond of fearless fellowship with him; human life becomes a struggle of toil and pain. Sin once sown soon bears its hateful fruit of envy, murder, and all corruption. After many generations, at Yahweh's call, one goes forth from country and kindred in the east to the land of Canaan, there to receive revelations of the divine will and to enjoy fellowship with God in righteous and generous relations with man. The descendants of this man continued for many years in the land, reinforced by further kindred elements from the old home in Mesopotamia, until a portion of them go down into Egypt and dwell there.

The writers of Judah gathered traditions of many origins, but in our present study neither their source nor the amount of historical truth which they may preserve primarily concerns us. We are interested, rather, in the advance that the document shows its writers to have made upon the religious ideas of the century of the united kingdom.

The conception of God embodied in the narratives is in some aspects childlike indeed. He manipulates clay and shapes a man, breathing life into his nostrils; he walks and talks with men and comes down to earth to see what is being done by the builders at Babel. Yet, from the religious point of view, the heritage of Hebrew and general Semitic tradition is molded by ideas that show a great advance upon those of previous generations. Not only is God thought of as guiding human life in the formation of man and the course of human history, but his purposes include man's moral life. His obedient followers are characterized by hospitality to the stranger, self-sacrificing generosity to a younger relative when a conflict of interests arises, persistence in seeking the divine blessing, faithfulness to a human master, and respect for the marriage relation. For Joseph to be unfaithful and sin with his master's wife would be to commit "great wickedness and sin against God."

The old stories, it is true, do not show an appreciation of all the virtues that might be insisted upon by the later Hebrew prophets or Christian teachers. Abraham lies about his wife and does not dream of chivalrous protection, and the writer does not seem to count it a sin; Jacob exhibits some of the worst vices of his race and but few of its virtues, yet he seems to be the special object of divine care. Negative examples such as these indicate the undeveloped character of ethical thinking revealed by the narratives, but do not vitiate their general worth as giving positive pictures of primitive virtues most winsomely presented.

Continuing through the exodus period, this early strand of Hebrew history is the source for much of our knowledge of the work of Moses already considered. It contains a brief code of laws, in Exodus, chapter 34, which it seems to regard as the Decalogue written on the two tables; yet even this early collection of commands is of such a nature that it must have been formulated after the settlement in Canaan, so that it represents the legal side of religion a little later than the time of Moses. These laws deal with matters of cultus and not of morals; they limit worship to the one God, proscribe molten images, direct the observance of the seventh day, and the feasts of unleavened bread, of weeks, and of ingathering at the end

of the year, and deal with other similar matters.
As was indicated in chapter iii, some of these laws
would hardly be applicable to nomad life.

A genuine confidence in God's watchful care
and in his just judgments characterizes this document, which it is customary to style the Judean
prophetic history. It is justly counted as a part of
the prophetic literature of the nation and shows
how men of prophetic spirit, in the ninth century
before Christ, interpreted God's character and
will as revealed in human history.

A generation or two after the composition of the
Judean history men of the Northern Kingdom,
who were akin in spirit to the Judean writers, made
a compilation of early traditions with less of
emphasis upon Judah and more upon the tribes of
the north. Their interest and purpose were not so
broadly historical as those of the Judean writers,
being centered even more upon the religious aspects
of the past. The dominant personalities through
whom God exercised his guidance and the methods
of God's communication with them are of supreme
interest to these writers.

The writers of the north had advanced consider-
ably in their theological thinking beyond those of
the Judean history. Bald anthropomorphisms
have been removed from the stories; such scenes
as the coming down of the Deity to the Garden,
Babel, or Sodom, and the wrestling of Jacob at

Penuel, have generally disappeared. God, instead, reveals himself through angelic messengers or dreams.

Some of the less worthy moral aspects of the stories have also vanished or been modified; Abraham's misrepresentation concerning Sarah is explained on the ground that she was indeed his sister, the daughter of the same father, though not of the same mother. To us this may not seem to mitigate his conduct, but it does seem to show some dawning consciousness on the part of the narrator that a great religious hero ought not to be guilty of falsehood. In Abraham's treatment of Hagar and Jacob's questionable dealings with Laban the responsibility is thrown back upon the Deity, for Abraham does not expel Hagar until he receives a command, and God's intervention rather than Jacob's cunning is the cause of Laban's worsting.

A notable advance is suggested by the story of the golden calf in Exodus, which seems to indicate that this mode of representing Yahweh is condemned at the time of composition, a century and a half after Jeroboam's setting up of the golden calves at Dan and Bethel. The great prominence of prophets and the emphasis upon their leadership of the people in paths of blessing, together with the whole spirit of the document, fully justify the description of it as the Ephraimite prophetic history.

This history contained a much longer law code than the Decalogue of Exodus, chap. 34, which was referrred to above. This second collection of laws, now found in Exodus 20:22—23:19, is commonly styled the Book of the Covenant; it includes the ritual laws of chapter 34, a considerable body of case laws dealing with civil matters (21:1—22:16), and miscellaneous commands concerning both worship and social duties. In the matter of worship, sacrifice to Yahweh in various places is presupposed, in contrast to the insistence of Israel's later law that such worship must be limited to Jerusalem alone. However, the recognition of any other deities is so drastically proscribed that one feels that the code must have been influenced by Elijah's struggle against the Tyrian Baal and the reform which followed—anyone sacrificing to another god is to be utterly destroyed and the names of other gods must not even be spoken.

The laws dealing with social relations mark a great advance upon anything we have previously noted in the moral ideals of Israel's religion. Not only do these regulations denounce such matters as false witness and wrongs done to the poor and unprotected members of the community; they provide that the owners of the land shall leave its fruits for the poor one year in seven, that every seventh day shall be granted to servant and beast of burden for rest, and that active kindness shall be shown even to one's enemy.

Peters well suggests that these prophetic histories "bore the same relation to the actual religion of the people which the works of a few spiritual-minded thinkers, chiefly monks, bore to the actual religion of the mass of the people in Italy or France or Germany or England in the Dark Ages." Their composition does, however, indicate that certain men, probably considerable schools of men, in both Israel and Judah, were progressively attaining and trying to spread among their countrymen high ideals of the divine movement in history and of the character of God and of his followers. They show, too, that these thinkers had gone very far along the road from early Semitic polytheism toward monotheism.

In view of the fact that Elijah and the writing prophets of the following era appear usually alone and in opposition to all that prevails in the religious and moral practices of the people, and even in opposition to most men belonging to the prophetic order, it is especially significant to find in the prophetic histories of the two kingdoms evidence that there was progress in the ethical religious thinking of Israel which found effective expression in the writings of the groups of unnamed historians of both kingdoms.

SUPPLEMENTARY READING

Budde, *Religion of Israel to the Exile*, pp. 104–22.

H. P. Smith, *The Religion of Israel*, pp. 82–87, 90–116.

Peters, *The Religion of the Hebrews*, pp. 158–69, 174–95.

Peake, *The Religion of Israel*, pp. 43–51.

Marti, *Religion of the Old Testament*, pp. 116–23.

Ottley, *The Religion of Israel*, pp. 60–66.

Addis, *Hebrew Religion*, pp. 78–134 (treats together the periods covered by this chapter and the previous one).

CHAPTER V

THE GOD OF JUSTICE AND LOVE

References for study—

    (1) Amos 7:10–17.
    (2) Amos, chaps. 1, 2.
    (3) Amos, chaps. 3, 4, 5; 8:1–10.
    (4) Hos. 1:1–9; 2:2—3:5.
    (5) Hos. 4:1–10; 6:1–10; chap. 11.

Note in (1) the circumstances of Amos' preaching and his relation to the prophetic order; in (2) the application of principles of justice to international and economic affairs; in (3) the ground of Israel's responsibility, the social evils of the times, and the prophet's substitute for empty ritual; in (4) Hosea's personal experience and its application to Israel; in (5) the social conditions and the prophet's conception of God's relation to Israel.

Our previous study has led to rather broad and general conceptions, based often upon fragmentary evidence, sometimes of uncertain date. With the middle of the eighth century B.C. we come to a very different kind of standing-ground. The great religious teachers of Israel now begin to preserve their sermons and songs in separate books which have come down to us in something like their original form. The history of Israel's religious progress becomes the life-story of these teachers. Through them streams of religious thinking, which

have long been gathering, suddenly emerge, making
the age one of the most important eras in the moral
and religious history of humanity.   In the oracles
of these prophet-teachers we are able to see the
times in which they live and the personal experiences through which they are led to new levels
of religious insight.   Thus our study becomes
largely biographical for the two centuries of the
prophetic age.

Four great names, Amos, Hosea, Isaiah, and
Micah, mark the brief half-century that brings the
Hebrew revelation of God and of human duty
almost to its culminating point.   The first two of
these appear in Northern Israel, where Elijah had
done his work more than a century before.

Amos is a second and greater Elijah, and, like
his prototype, he stands amid the scenes of wealth
and luxury of the larger kingdom as one who comes
from simpler and sterner surroundings.   Elijah
came from the grazing districts east of the Jordan,
Amos from among the herdsmen of Tekoa, a
mountain-top village on the borders of the wilderness in Southern Judea.   Suddenly he steps forth,
a stern figure in shepherd garb, and startles the gay
throngs at the royal sanctuary of Bethel.

He begins with a song or poetic oracle of doom.

> Yahweh from Zion shall roar,
> From Jerusalem utter his voice,
> The shepherd's pastures shall mourn
> The crest of Carmel wither.

His swift-flashing pictures sweep about the borders of Canaan from Syria to the other ancient foes—Philistia, Ammon, Moab—denouncing each in turn for some act of cruelty in warfare known to his hearers. With the skill of a supreme orator he carries his auditors with him by starting on a road that they will gladly travel. Doom upon their foes for cruel acts committed against Israel, expressed in majestic, rhythmic speech, could not fail to win a sympathetic hearing.

Then the prophet leads on to the thought that Israel's God condemns Moab also for an act of wanton vengeance against the dead king of Edom. Here he takes a great step forward in assuming that the God of Israel is concerned with the treatment which other nations accord one another. Yahweh becomes thus a God of nations holding the balances between them in righteousness. If Amos is not thus a thoroughgoing monotheist, he certainly oversteps the bounds of absolute henotheism; but he is not concerned with such distinctions. His purpose is to secure assent to the principle that God must punish selfish, cruel conduct wherever it raises its ugly head. With this assumed he hastens to apply his principle to Israel, for the men of Israel have been passing cruel to their own poor and unjust to their unfortunate.

The application so skilfully introduced represents the precise opposite of the hearers' faith.

The time is one of great national prosperity. The
ancient struggle with Damascus had been brought
to a close, a generation before, by Syria's complete
humiliation before the advance of the great military
power of the day, Assyria. Then, for a time,
Assyria's westward campaigns had been checked
by her own internal troubles, and the reigning king
of Israel, Jeroboam II, had been able to spread his
boundaries rapidly, bringing under his sway many
of the surrounding peoples. Wealth had grown
with conquest. According to the ancient doctrine
of the people, God had shown his satisfaction by
thus blessing the nation. They were looking, not
for judgment, but for greater manifestations of his
will and power to make his people prosperous.

In subsequent addresses Amos presents in
varied ways his new and epoch-making doctrine
that Yahweh's choice of Israel was ground for her
greater condemnation, and that his blessing was
conditional upon the social righteousness of the
people. If the merchant sold refuse wheat and
dealt with false weights and measures, if the elders
who sat at the village gate as a local court of justice
accepted bribes from rich litigants and turned
aside the poor from his right, if the wealthy women
caused their husbands to crush the needy in order
that they might enjoy their wine suppers, then the
nation could not be the object of God's favor but
must soon meet just condemnation and ruin.

No teacher of the pre-Christian era, it is safe to say, comes so close to the most vital interests of our twentieth century as this prophet of the eighth century before Christ. The attack which he makes upon bribery and the oppression of the poor has been re-echoed again and again in recent years among all the more advanced nations of the world, where the struggle for political equality has passed on to the struggle for honest government and economic justice. With the transference of interest from such questions to the strife of nation against nation, when war breaks out, appeal is made to God for national victory, and many deny that the principles of righteousness can be applied in the dealings of nations. At such a time the voice of Amos rings out anew, declaring that God demands righteous dealing of nation with nation as well as of class with class. Yahweh's previous blessing upon a people imposes a far greater responsibility than rests upon others to let justice roll down as waters and righteousness as a mighty stream.

The opening years of the twentieth century as possibly no previous fifteen years of history have made it possible to appreciate the outreach of faith and doctrine. Many who acknowledge the God of Amos and of Christ shrink back from the audacious certitude of the ancient prophet's belief that God's unwavering test of a nation is the justice of its political and economic life and of its relations with other peoples.

In tracing the religious history of Israel Amos is significant not only for his own great contribution to the advance of religious thought, but also for the contemporary evidence which his book affords as to the prevalent ideas and practices of the people. We have already noted that the people interpreted national prosperity as the mark of divine favor and as an earnest of even greater blessings. The "day of Yahweh," the day when he should especially manifest himself for his people, was the object of their longing desire. The book indicates also that worship was conducted not only at Bethel and Dan, but also at Gilgal and, apparently, at Samaria and Beersheba. Freewill-offerings, thank-offerings of leavened bread, burnt-offerings, peace-offerings of fat beasts, and tithes were all brought to the sanctuaries where the sound of musical instrument and song arose in honor of Yahweh.

The new moon and the Sabbath alike were observed as days of abstinence from buying and selling. Apparently the lands outside of Canaan were accounted ceremonially unclean, although the old Canaanite worship of license with wine and harlotry still existed in Israel, the Nazarites were led to break their vows of abstinence from wine, and the prophets were forbidden to speak.

Such are the outstanding features in the picture
of Israel's religion given by Amos about the year
750 B.C. The people are not irreligious; they have
faith in the power and purpose of their God to
prosper his people; they worship him with a varied
and liberal ceremonial. Some forms connected
with the worship may have an idolatrous character,
but, in the main and so far as it goes, it seems in
accord with the practices approved in the later law
codes. To Amos the very sumptuousness of the
service, in contrast with the absence of sacrificial
ceremony in the wilderness period, is an offense;
but his chief ground of condemnation of the worship is that Yahweh's true service consists in
righteous conduct rather than in song and sacrifice.

Now for the first time in our study the line
between the priestly and the prophetic sides of
religion becomes clearly marked. In the earliest
times priest and prophet had essentially the same
function, namely, to discover the unknown for the
people whether by interpreting the omens from the
organs of the sacrificial victim, casting the sacred
lot, falling into a prophetic frenzy, or whatever
the particular means of ascertaining the divine
will and purpose might be. Gradually, with the
development of the ceremonial side of religion,
there came to be an organized priesthood which
alone could officiate at the sacrifices and which
developed and preserved an approved system of

ceremonial. From the priestly function of interpreting the omens and casting the lot there grew
up a body of decisions that formed the priestly
Torah, "teaching" or "law," which will be discussed in a later chapter.

The true prophets, freeing themselves from the
primitive practices of gazers and seers with their
trances, came to understand more and more of the
divine nature and purposes and to interpret life
and history in the light of their increasing knowledge of Yahweh's character. As their appreciation
of God's essentially moral character grew clearer
and clearer they must inevitably come into conflict
with all that opposed the moral interpretation of
life as affording the supreme standard.

With Amos the issue became sharply drawn and
acute. Justice in business and government, and
not burnt-offerings or hymns, was his interpretation of God's will for man. To the established
priest of Bethel the prophet was but a "seer" or
"gazer," seeking a living by plying his trade at the
king's sanctuary. To this implication of belonging to the order of professional prophets Amos
answered with vehement denial, claiming a special
mission from Yahweh. The scene at the Bethel
sanctuary thus distinguishes the member of a
prophetic order from the specially commissioned
prophet almost as sharply as it distinguishes
prophet from priest.

Near the close of the same prosperous reign of Jeroboam II Hosea became conscious that the experiences of his life had been God's leading along a dark path to a sublime truth which he must now proclaim. The opening chapters of his book tell, in brief and broken utterances, the tragic story of his domestic life. The personal experience is so fused with its interpretation and application to Israel that it is not always easy to distinguish where the prophet is speaking of himself, his wife, and her lovers, and where of Yahweh, Israel, and the Baalim. Very probably the outward facts of Hosea's history were familiar to his hearers so that they would understand all the circumstances more readily than we can do.

This seems to be the essence of Hosea's tragedy: He married one Gomer, the daughter of Diblaim, betrothing her to him in purity as Yahweh won Israel in the wilderness. He was a man of insight who already understood that the bloody methods adopted by Jehu in stamping out the house of Ahab and the baalism which it supported deserved a prophetic condemnation, and so he named his eldest son Jezreel as a sign that the blood spilt there would return upon the house of Jehu. To his second child, a daughter, the prophet gave the ominous name "She is not pitied," indicative of God's determined judgment upon Israel. To the third child he gave the name "Not my people," for

Israel had ceased to be God's people.   Now Gomer
had left her husband for a paramour, and Hosea
in his indignation denied that she was his wife and
would have no mercy upon her children.

Apparently the woman's course led, at length,
to its natural issue and, deserted of her lovers, she
fell into actual slavery.   Hosea still loved her and
bought her from her owner; many days she should
abide for him no man's wife and so would he be
also toward her.

In taking back his faithless wife to the protection
of his house Hosea realized that Yahweh thus
loved his people, though they turned to other gods.
In the period of purifying discipline through which
Gomer must pass he saw the necessity of Israel's
exile in which she must abide long without the
sacred pillar that stood beside Canaanite and
Hebrew altars, without image, and without sacrifice, the visible means by which she sought fellowship with Deity.

Through this tragic experience Hosea felt that
God had called him to pass in order that he might
know and understand.   Amos had comprehended
Yahweh's justice and had seen that condemnation
must fall upon all unrighteousness.   Hosea was no
less conscious of impending doom, but his inner
experience had taught him that although God must
discipline, his love was unchangeable.   On one
occasion he pictured the relation of God and Israel

as that of a father and tenderly cherished son who had grown up to waywardness.

As in Amos, so in Hosea it is God's care of his people in bringing them from the land of Egypt to which appeal is made. A study of the work of these prophets places us in a better position than at first to realize the significance of the exodus as the basis for the moral appeal in Israel's religion. The God who had compassion upon the people in their misery, in the helplessness of their childhood, could arouse them to compassion toward men and gratitude toward him if anything could do so.

Amos' message, however, must end in hopeless doom upon a people who had flouted the divine watch-care, while Hosea's heart teaches him that one who truly loves can never wholly give up the loved one: "How shall I give thee up, Ephraim? how shall I cast thee off, Israel? my heart is turned within me, my compassions are kindled together. I will not execute the fierceness of mine anger, I will not return to destroy Ephraim: for I am God, and not man." The prophet's thought swings between the hopelessness of his people's condition, who perish for lack of knowledge, and the unchanging love that cannot abandon them to their just fate. Love itself is helpless to save when there is no comprehension and response, yet the divine love remains a ground of hope.

Hosea goes much more deeply to the roots of life, its doom and its salvation, than Amos can do. His message will be taken up and carried on to fuller insight by Jeremiah, but will reach its consummation only in the teaching of Jesus as interpreted in the Fourth Gospel. There the true nature and meaning of religion finds its final solution in the thought that eternal life is comprehending fellowship between the Father and his children, fellowship, too, of the children with one another in the great family. There Hosea's despairing realization that the people perish because they do not know God as the loving, faithful husband or father is answered by the elder son, who is the express image of the father, through whom the younger sons come to know God and enter into sympathetic fellowship with him.

If Amos' message is epoch-making in human history as revealing the only firm warp and woof out of which a harmonious and lasting economic, political, and social fabric can be woven for this world, Hosea's message carries us far beyond this, introducing us to that ultimate interpretation of life in terms of the family which holds true not only for this world, but for the next as well, transforming this life even into the eternal life of the divine family as well as into an ordered society.

The corrupting character of the existing religion is pictured again and again by Hosea in vivid terms: "Whoredom and wine and new wine take away the understanding. My people ask counsel at their stock, and their staff declareth unto them; for the spirit of whoredom hath caused them to err, and they have played the harlot, departing from under their God. They sacrifice upon the tops of the mountains, and burn incense upon the hills, under oaks and poplars and terebinths, because the shadow thereof is good: therefore your daughters play the harlot, and your brides commit adultery. I will not punish your daughters when they play the harlot, nor your brides when they commit adultery; for the men themselves go apart with harlots, and they sacrifice with the prostitutes; and the people that doth not understand shall be overthrown" (4:11–14). Images of gold and silver have been made and idolatry has become prevalent, yet the people make their sacrifices to Yahweh (8:4, 11, 13).

Whether Hosea's picture of the company of priests lying in wait to murder like troops of robbers is a literal or only a figurative description of rapaciousness, in any case it vividly presents the corruption of the priestly order in the later years of Hosea's ministry, a time when the strong rule of Jeroboam had been followed by a succession of assassinations and complete anarchy. It was a time when the thief entered in and the troop of robbers ravaged without.

Amos would substitute for elaborate ritual just dealings in all life's relations. Hosea imaginatively pictures Ephraim penitent for the moment, seeking to return to Yahweh, and assures the people that what God desires is kindness and not sacrifice, and knowledge of himself rather than burnt-offerings. Both prophets appear opposed to priestly ritual as the true practice of religion, whether the ritual be counted as Yahweh-worship or is so intermingled with Canaanite ideas and usages as to be practical idolatry.

In offering a substitute for forms of worship, each is true to his own apprehension of God's essential nature. Yet there is no contradiction between their two conceptions of God and of his service. One conceives him as just and desiring that the strong shall do justice to the weak; the other conceives him as loving and longing that his people shall do kindness one to another. A God who was mighty and just without love would be an object of terror and would not lay such stress upon the wrongs of the poor and weak as Amos' God does. A God who was loving without justice would be a partial respecter of persons, a corrupting influence, and would not lay such stress upon the corruption of the political and religious order and its inevitable doom as Hosea's God does. Each prophet is able to see distinctly different aspects of the same infinite perfection, and each has his significant contribution to make toward Israel's completed revelation of God.

Less than fifteen years elapsed between the last recorded words of Hosea and the capture of Samaria with the downfall of Northern Israel. The promise of religion in the north was great; hence had come Deborah, Samuel, Elijah, the authors of the Ephraimite prophetic history, and Hosea, and here, too, Amos had delivered his only recorded oracles; but the national life of the Northern Kingdom came to an abrupt end and its religious message was passed over to the sister-kingdom by which it was preserved, developed, and handed on to future generations.

SUPPLEMENTARY READING

Peake, *The Religion of Israel*, pp. 52–68.

Addis, *Hebrew Religion*, pp. 135–69.

Budde, *Religion of Israel to the Exile*, pp. 122–41.

H. P. Smith, *The Religion of Israel*, pp. 131–46.

Peters, *The Religion of the Hebrews*, pp. 205–25.

Ottley, *The Religion of Israel*, pp. 67–90 (treats the eighth-century prophets together).

Marti, *Religion of the Old Testament*, pp. 124–83 (treats the prophets as a whole).

Badè, *The Old Testament in the Light of To-Day*, pp. 132–66.

CHAPTER VI

THE EXALTED GOD OF NATIONS

References for study—

(1) Isa. chap. 6; 1:4; 2:17; 5:16; 6:1–4.

(2) Isa. 1:10–17; 3:13–26; 5:1–12, 18–23; 9:13–17; 28:7–11.

(3) II Kings, chap. 16; Isa. 7:1–20; 28:1–4; 20:1–6; 39:1–8; 36:1–10, 21–22; 37:1–4; 29:15–16; 30:1–17; 31:1–4.

(4) Isa. 10:5–19; 23:9.

(5) Isa. 4:2–4; 6:13; 7:3; 17:4–6; 28:5.

(6) Isa. 11:1–9; 32:1–8, 15–18; 19:23–25.

(7) Isa. 10:24–34; 14:24–27, 32; 29:1–8; 31:45.

(8) Mic. 2:1–2; 3:1–3, 9–11.

(9) Mic. 3:5, 7, 11.

(10) Mic. 3:12; cf. Jer. 26:17–19.

(11) Mic. 6:1–8.

Note in group (1) the steps in Isaiah's inner experience and the attributes of God; in (2) the social and economic conditions as compared with Amos' picture of Northern Israel, the moral blindness compared with Hosea's conception of perishing for lack of knowledge, and the condemnation of false leaders; in (3) the international crises and Isaiah's policy; in (4) the conception of God's use of human motives and condemnation of that which exalts itself; in (5) the doctrine of the remnant; in (6) the hope; in (7) the inviolability of Zion; in (8) the social and economic conditions as seen by a peasant prophet of the Judean hills;

in (9) religious conditions; in (10) Micah's announcement
of judgment and its effect; in (11) the dramatic presentation of the prophetic demands.

Isaiah's ministry began in Jerusalem shortly
before the close of Hosea's work in Northern Israel.
The record of the inaugural vision from which we
date the opening of the great prophet's labors was
doubtless written years after the event, when later
experiences had become fused in memory with the
convictions of this early time, yet the narrative
gives one of the simplest and clearest accounts of
a profound religious experience ever recorded.

In an earlier chapter of this book we noted the
fact that the great prophets of Israel were relatively free from ecstatic visions and all such phenomena, but this does not mean that they did not
have mystic experience of the divine presence and
illumination.   Indeed, it would be difficult to
name any of the greatest religious leaders of history who have not known something of genuine
vision experience. Amos, Isaiah, Jeremiah, and
Ezekiel all record their visions. Paul was caught
up even to the third heaven, whether in the body
or out of the body he did not know. Savonarola,
Luther, and many lesser Christian teachers illus-
trate the general truth, and even Jesus himself told
his followers in symbolic vision of the temptation
that preceded his active ministry. Outside of the
Hebrew and Christian religions the phenomena

are equally characteristic of other religions. The student of Mahomet's life, for example, cannot question the sincerity of the prophet's conviction of direct divine communication in the earlier days of his ministry.

In all cases of unusual religious excitement it is exceedingly difficult to distinguish the genuine from the spurious. At one extreme we find the ancient priests of Baal cutting themselves, leaping upon the altar, and calling upon their god from morning till evening, the shouting and whirling dervishes of Mohammedanism, or the ignorant adherents of Christianity counting a cataleptic condition as possession by the Deity. At the other extreme we see the exceptional experience of the loftiest souls, to whom there has been given from a power outside themselves direct vision of that which eye hath not seen nor ear heard.

The best test of the validity of such unusual experience is its effect upon the mind and life. To the Corinthians, who were ambitious for the ecstatic gift of tongues, Paul commended speech easy to be understood and speaking with tongues only when it could be interpreted. Similarly we may apply his standard of edifying, that is, building up, to recorded visions. Has the vision truth that can be applied in daily life? Does it lead to higher and more devoted living, or is it an end in itself, a means of self-glorification? With the greatest religious leaders the visions that come are infrequent. Paul looked back more than fourteen years to his, and Isaiah and Jeremiah record such experiences only at the opening of their long ministries.

Examining Isaiah's vision in detail, we find that it contains an overwhelming apprehension of the exalted God which dominated all the prophet's long years of devoted labor and constituted his chief contribution to Israel's conception of God. The song of the seraphim was "Holy, holy, holy," and henceforth the prophet's favorite name for God is the Holy One of Israel. The Hebrew word "holy," *kadosh*, is but another form of the root that we have met in the wilderness Kadesh, "Sanctuary." Its earliest significance is probably separation or withdrawal, but in Isaiah's vision God's separation from man seems to have the moral element in it, "for the uncleanness of the lips must refer to sinful utterance."

The glory of this God which fills the whole earth is not simply the glory of exaltation and separation, it is a quality which makes Isaiah conscious of his own sin and the need of the people among whom he dwells: "Woe is me! for I am undone; because I am a man of unclean lips and I dwell in the midst of a people of unclean lips: for mine eyes have seen the King." It is only when his own offending lips have been purified by a coal from the altar that

Isaiah is ready to hear the call, "Whom shall I send and who will go for us?" and to answer, "Here am I; send me."

In the earlier writings of Israel we have found no such universalism as that implied in the song of the seraphim and no such conception of God's holiness. To the justice and love of God that Amos and Hosea had apprehended, Isaiah adds holiness and the thought that the glory of this God fills the whole earth.

Testing the vision by the questions: How does it affect the seer's mind and life? Has it truth applicable to the lives of others? we find in this vision the shaping of a great life and an experience such as has led to many another life of service. A vision of God that reveals first one's own sin and then the need and call of one's generation, and leads on to devoted, wise service is genuine; if such a vision enlarges for all time man's view of God's universality and of his holiness, it may be counted a true revelation.

In the clear light that shone from the face of the exalted, holy God, Isaiah saw and denounced the economic evils of his day with even more power than Amos commanded. The princes who crushed the people and ground the face of the poor; the wealthy landowners who joined house to house and laid field to field until they dwelt alone on their great estates, absorbing the holdings of the small, independent farmers; the haughty women of Jerusalem mincing through the streets with wanton eyes; the feasters who tarried long at the wine, but regarded not the work of the Lord—all these are denounced most scathingly in Isaiah's early sermons.

The prophet's attack upon growing land monopoly shows that he comprehends the fundamental problem of a state that is economically healthy; but he goes deeper than economic conditions into the heart of man when he denounces those who call evil good and good evil, that put darkness for light and light for darkness, that say to the prophets, "Prophesy not unto us right things, speak unto us smooth things." As in Hosea's sense of the people's one vital need, so in this flash of insight reaching to the roots of life, the world must wait for a fuller interpretation until Jesus of Nazareth shall reveal life; it was only those who called good evil and evil good, who seeing deeds of divine compassion called them the work of Satan, of whom he despaired. Upon such Isaiah had pronounced woe, and all experience shows such moral perversity to be the great obstacle to man's spiritual progress.

Isaiah had opportunity to apply his religious principles to the foreign policy of his nation through a succession of crises in which the future was most obscure and party differences ran high. Soon

after the inaugural vision a coalition of Israel and
Damascus threatened Judah, probably wishing to
force her into an alliance against Assyria. In
alarm Ahaz determined to call in the help of
Assyria and, in doing so, purchased immediate
release at the price of making his nation tributary
to Assyria. Northern Israel suffered partial
depopulation and the loss of much of its territory
at this time, and, a dozen years later, its capital,
Samaria, was captured and a large part of its inhabitants deported. Judah for the time remained loyal
to Assyria and escaped serious trouble, but later
King Hezekiah received a deputation from Mero-
dach Baladan of Babylon, who was plotting revolt
against his Assyrian overlord; some four years
after this Judah, relying upon Egypt for help, was
herself in revolt against Assyria.

Through all these complex events, in which little
Judah was feeling the full force of her position as
one of the small buffer states between the great
seats of power to the east and west of her, Isaiah
appears constantly as political adviser of king
and people. Sometimes his advice was sought;
more often it was given undesired. His fundamental principle became clear in the first great
crisis—Trust God and avoid entangling alliances.
After Ahaz had sought assistance from Assyria,
however, Isaiah's advice was consistently to remain true to that agreement and to avoid all

negotiations with Assyria's enemies whether in Egypt or Babylon.

It may have been Isaiah's influence that kept Judah from compromising herself at the time of Samaria's destruction. Whether this is the case or not, twenty years later his influence was completely overridden by the party that favored Egyptian alliance, and Jerusalem was brought to the verge of destruction. At this crisis, when the Assyrian army had swept over the country and no human power could save the capital city, Isaiah stood forth strong in his assured faith that Yahweh would not permit the city to be captured, and gave expression to his doctrine of the inviolability of Zion.

The issue justified the prophet's faith, for the main body of the Assyrian army met some mysterious calamity, probably the outbreak of a pestilence, on the borders of Egypt, and suddenly withdrew from Palestine. The vindication of Isaiah's faith must have given him greater influence than he had ever known before; it certainly led to the fixing of the nation's faith that Jerusalem could never be captured. A hundred years later another prophet needed to combat this doctrine with all the force possible.

Another aspect of Isaiah's conception of God's working in international events is seen in his teaching that Assyria, in its cruel lust for destruction,

was but the rod in Yahweh's hand used to smite
faithless Samaria and Jerusalem. God, he was
sure, would in time visit judgment upon the self-
exalted king of Assyria. Isaiah's emphasis upon
the exaltation of God involved ever the corollary
that all that exalts itself must be brought low.
Arrogance seemed to him, hardly less than to
Aeschylus among the Greeks, sure precursor of
condemnation and fall.

We thus find Isaiah thinking out much more
fully than Amos the complex problem of the divine
rule among the nations. Amos had pronounced
absolute doom upon Northern Israel in the name
of the God of justice, and had hinted at distant
Assyria as the instrument of destruction; Isaiah
taught that cruel, self-confident Assyria must
suffer judgment in turn, and he always found hope
for the ultimate deliverance of his own people or
of a purified remnant of the people. This doctrine
of a remnant is one of the most frequently expressed
teachings of the Book of Isaiah and is a fruitful
source of the ineradicable hope of future generations
of Isaiah's people.

The hope found in the volume of this great
prophet's oracles does not limit itself to the saving
of a purged remnant; it reaches out to lofty antici-
pations of an ideal ruler of the house of David,
upon whom the spirit of Yahweh shall rest, the
spirit of wisdom and understanding, the spirit of

counsel and might, the spirit of knowledge and of
the fear of Yahweh, a ruler who shall judge the
poor righteously. Out of the age of struggle
between Assyria and Egypt in which Judah was
well-nigh torn to shreds the prophet looked to a
future day when the contending nations should
worship together, with Israel a blessing between
them.

Many scholars count these wonderful visions
of the future as insertions in the Book of Isaiah,
expressing a faith which reached such full development only generations after Isaiah's time. Even
if this is the case, the later editors who placed
these among the original oracles of the eighth-
century prophet did so with the justification that
the roots of the hope which find such splendid
flowering are to be traced to Isaiah who, in his
youth, saw the exalted God whose glory filled the
earth, and in the strength of that vision was able
to see, through the long years of conflict and devastation, the sure purposes of God's mercy to his
people.

Even in the struggle of the nations Isaiah's
vision of God revealed to him just and beneficent
purpose. When his own wisdom was flouted, his
party defeated in the nation's counsel, and, in
consequence, the enemies were at the gate, his
faith never faltered. The unquestionably historic
facts of Isaiah's ministry may well justify belief

that some at least of the most exalted hopes
expressed in the book which bears his name were
his genuine utterances.

While Isaiah was working among the noble
and wealthy in Jerusalem, the prophet Micah
was among the peasant farmers on the western
slope of the Judean hills, some twenty miles west
of Amos' home. Here the building up of the
great estates which Isaiah had pictured was
keenly felt. Micah knew from the viewpoint of
the common people the terrible results of the
haste to be rich that was corrupting church and
state.

When Amaziah, priest of Bethel, intimated that
Amos was prophesying as a means of livelihood, the
herdsman of Tekoa stoutly denied that he was a professional prophet. The reason for his attitude may
become clearer as we read Micah's description of
the prophets of Judah, "that make the people to
err; that bite with their teeth and cry, Peace;
and whoso putteth not into their mouths, they
even prepare war against him." Professional
prophets and priests alike seemed to this champion
of the suffering poor to be as mercenary and corrupt
as the civil rulers and capitalists of the day.
Though such spokesmen of God as Elijah, Isaiah,
Amos, and Hosea had raised prophecy to incom-
parable moral heights, there were evidently seers
and prophets in large numbers who were on much

the same level as the common soothsayers and
diviners of other religions.

All four of the great eighth-century prophets
appear within one generation and with a message
that is singularly unified, yet each has his own distinct emphasis and way of expressing truth, and
they stand forth a lone group against a sordid
background of priests who see nothing in religion
except ceremonial worship and the living this
provides for them, and prophets whose vision
is determined by the silver that crosses their
palms.

Lonely as the true prophets seem to stand, like
towering summits which have caught the rays of
a new day while mists and shadows and all lurking
things are still abroad in the valleys, they must
have reflected their light to many who treasured
their truths; how else were their writings preserved through all the vicissitudes of subsequent
centuries?

The members of the group, although they lived
and taught in different districts, seem to have some
knowledge of the words of the others who have
spoken before them. Near the close of the Book of
Micah the threefold demand of Amos, Hosea, and
Isaiah is preserved in perfect summary and with
all the appeal of dramatic imagination. The
prophet as herald gives Yahweh's summons to a
great assize, where the majestic mountains are to

be the judges in his impeachment of Israel. God himself then speaks, not in the thunderclap of Sinai, but in the more divine tones of tender pleading, reminding his people of their deliverance from bondage, of his guidance of them through the wilderness, and of their safe passage of the Jordan. Led to penitence by these memories the people ask what they may bring as suitable offering to such a God. Will the gifts of royal wealth, thousands of rams, or, of wildest imagination, ten thousands of rivers of oil, or, more precious than all, the first-born child—will these be suitable return for the divine benefits received? In startling contrast to all this the prophet answers: "He hath showed thee, O man, what is good; and what doth the Lord require of thee but to do justly and to love kindness and to walk humbly with thy God?"

Here speak again Amos, who conceived God first of all as just; Hosea, who came to know God as of tender compassion; Isaiah, who saw God exalted in holiness and man utterly corrupt before him. In this winnowed truth from his three great predecessors Micah gave to the world one of the most perfect expressions of man's duty to man and God ever framed in human speech. Indeed, it stands alone in its perfection until the two commands of love, on which hang all the law and the prophets, are united.

SUPPLEMENTARY READING

Peake, *The Religion of Israel*, pp. 69–81.

Addis, *Hebrew Religion*, pp. 167–80.

Budde, *Religion of Israel to the Exile*, pp. 142–60.

H. P. Smith, *The Religion of Israel*, pp. 147–61.

Peters, *The Religion of the Hebrews*, pp. 226–41.

Ottley, *The Religion of Israel*, pp. 67–90 (treats the eighth-century prophets together).

Marti, *Religion of the Old Testament*, pp. 124–83 (treats the prophets as a whole).

Badè, *The Old Testament in the Light of To-Day*, pp. 167–86.

CHAPTER VII

RELIGION AND LAW

References for study—

- (1) II Kings 18:1–8; 21:1–9, 16–26.
- (2) Zeph. 1:4–6, 12; 3:4; Jer. 2:28; 5:19.
- (3) II Kings 22:1—23:30.
- (4) Deut. 12:1–28.
- (5) Deut. 17:2–5; 18:10–11.
- (6) Deut. 16:9–19; 22:1–4, 8; 24:14–15, 17–22; 26:12.
- (7) Deut. 5:6–21; cf. Exod. 20:1–17.
- (8) Deut. 6:4–5; 7:6–11; 8:3, 17–20; 10:12–19.

Note in (1) the specific evils which Hezekiah attempted to overthrow and those which Manasseh fostered; in (2) the religious conditions in the early years of Josiah; in (3) the specific evils which Josiah attempted to overthrow; in (4) the centralization of worship with provision that meat may be killed and eaten away from altar; in (5) the evil practices condemned; in (6) the spirit of justice and kind-ness; in (7) the differences in the two forms of the Deca-logue; in (8) the nature of Yahweh and his relations with Israel.

Isaiah's faith that Yahweh would not suffer his city and temple to be captured was remarkably vindicated when, in the year 701, the hosts of Sennacherib suddenly withdrew from Palestine. Hezekiah the king and the people, too, must now have been much under the influence of the great

Jerusalem prophet who had stood calm in his confident faith when it was clear that no human hand
could deliver the land from its invaders. A brief
general statement in the narrative of Kings suggests a sweeping destruction at this time of the
places of worship outside of Jerusalem and of the
ancient Canaanite symbols associated with them.
Later conditions suggest that the destruction
could hardly have been as complete as this indicates, yet there can be no question of the gen-
uineness of Hezekiah's attempt to carry out the
will of God, as interpreted by Micah, as well as
by Isaiah.

Whatever may have been the reforms that
Hezekiah undertook and supported throughout the
remainder of his reign, they were nullified when
his son Manasseh entered upon his long years of
rule. He is credited with restoration of the old
Canaanitish practices and with the introduction
of some foreign ideas as well. Solomon had provided places of worship for his foreign wives hard
by Jerusalem. Ahab had added to Israel's tendency to recognize the old lords of the land or to
worship Yahweh after the manner of their cult,
the royal recognition of the Tyrian Baal. Manasseh introduced ideas and practices characteristic
of the more distant Euphrates valley, when he set
up altars for the gods of the heavenly bodies in the
courts of the temple.

28575

It was customary in ancient Babylonia to arrange the images of the deities of conquered peoples as a kind of court of subject princes about the god of a victorious city. Some such idea as this may have been in Manasseh's mind when he introduced altars of other gods into the temple courts, but these were the gods of the race to which he was subject, and it seems, rather, that he sought to secure the favor of Assyria and her gods in addition to that of his own deity, whose deliverance during Hezekiah's reign had not assured the independence of Judah for many years.

It is very difficult to maintain pure henotheism in the vicissitudes of international conflicts. When one's own people are in dire need and the followers of other gods are more numerous and mightier, it seems prudent to seek the favor of these gods as well as of one's own. Manasseh seems to have been very cosmopolitan in his selection, if we are right in inferring from the name of his son Amon that he recognized the Egyptian god of this name as well as the lords of Assyria and Babylonia.

From a relatively early time in the national history of Israel the effort had been made to suppress those who used the widespread practices of augury and enchantment to secure the favorable action of spirits. Ecstatic practices there might be among the accredited prophets of Yahweh, but the followers of his religion were early comparatively free from the chicanery and base dominance of those who practiced enchantment and claimed to be possessed by familiar spirits. All such debasing and misleading superstition was encouraged by Manasseh's fostering of Canaanitish worship and his introduction of foreign religious ideals.

Child sacrifice had been familiar to Israel ever since her settlement among the Canaanites, who practiced it so freely, and it had been adopted from time to time by men of Israel. The idea lying behind this practice may be a noble one—willingness to devote that which is dearest to the god. It is so pictured in the story of Abraham ready to sacrifice Isaac, and in Micah's dramatic presentation of penitent Israel questioning whether the most precious possession should be offered in expiation of the soul's sin.

The early Judean code in Exodus, provides that the first-born sons shall be redeemed, adopting the principle that all first-born belong to God, but modifying it in its application to human children. The story of Abraham's sacrifice told in the northern history is similar in its teaching, since the lamb is substituted for Isaac. It is clear that the religious consciousness of Israel could not abandon the deep-seated tendency to human sacrifice except on a theory of substitution. King Ahaz does not accept the theory and sacrifices his son in the fire. Micah's substitute of justice,

kindness, and humility was much less likely to be
acceptable than the more tangible one of the early
law. Manasseh's support of all debasing superstition was especially marked by the practice of
child sacrifice.

Allusions to current conditions in Zephaniah
and the earlier sermons of Jeremiah indicate that
Manasseh's religious eclecticism continued to prevail for some twenty years after his death. Prophetic messages from the very years of his reign
are almost lacking, probably because his welcome
to a large number of cults could not tolerate any
teachers who insisted on the exclusive recognition
of one God in Judah. Of the innocent blood which
he shed till he had filled Jerusalem, that of loyal
prophets may well have been a part. Late tradition recounts the sawing asunder of Isaiah, whose
life may have extended into the early years of
Manasseh's reign and then have been violently
ended. Micah probably continued to prophesy
until the early years of this tragic time.

To ambitious rulers eager to bring their nation
into full association with other peoples the exclusive demands of Yahweh as interpreted by the
great prophets from Elijah to Micah seemed hostile
to the state. To the people the prophetic insistence
on morality rather than religious rites now time-
honored must have seemed nothing short of
impious. The priests whose living depended upon

the abundance of sacrifices, of which they received a portion, and whose mercenary character had been so bitterly denounced by Micah, and the prophets who interpreted the divine purpose as a profession, found their livelihood threatened by the type of teaching given by Isaiah and Micah. Political policy, religious conservatism, and vested interests—three mighty forces in any age—were all opposed to the reforms undertaken by Hezekiah. Under Hezekiah's son Manasseh all these interests enjoyed a riot of revenge for their temporary restraint, and the reaction brought conditions worse than those which the prophets had attacked.

Still, as we noted in the last chapter, there must have been loyal followers of the great prophets who jealously treasured their sermons. If such men attempted to work in public, they were soon cut off. Among them there were some who believed that the worship of the one true God of Israel could be safeguarded by law. They would not attempt such an impossible thing as substituting justice, mercy, and humility for accustomed forms of worship. Rather, they would point out how such traits might be realized in the accustomed worship, modified and purified.

Filled with the ideals of the prophetic historians who in north and south had gathered the ancient traditions of their people into the two great histories that told the story of the rise of Israel as

Yahweh's peculiar people, and prizing, too, the brief codes of law that these histories embodied, these men set themselves to compose a complete legal manual for the everyday life of the Hebrews. This was designed to secure the recognition of the one righteous God in a purified sacrificial worship and to apply his principles to the duties of daily life.

They made the law code of Exodus, chapters 20 to 23, the basis of their work, embodying with it other legal matter that had been handed down orally or in writing and evolved altogether a noble code of law, admirably adapted to meet just the needs that had come to such complete dominance in the reign of Manasseh.

In one respect they felt forced to nullify what their basic code permitted, the erecting of altars to Yahweh in various places (Deuteronomy, chapter 12; Exodus 20:24). To earlier generations the worship of Yahweh in any place hallowed by his peculiar presence in the stories of the past, or even in the local high place of any village of his people, seemed the right and acceptable practice. Our study has shown that such local worship was likely to become confused with that of the baal of the place and was certainly saturated with the licentiousness of Canaanite nature-worship.

Despite the foreign cults which had been introduced into the temple at Jerusalem, it seemed to the compilers of the new code that worship here might be so controlled as to be kept pure, and so they limited sacrificial worship to the central sanctuary. This required provision for killing and eating meat away from the altar. In earlier times all eating of meat had been a sacrificial act, but now the only requirement made is that the blood shall be poured out on the earth as water.

Worship of any but the one God is to be stamped out by the death penalty, as Jehu had attempted to destroy worship of the Tyrian Baal and as Manasseh had suppressed the public activities of the Yahweh prophets. The laws are especially directed against the worship of sun and moon and all the host of heaven, and also against child sacrifice, divination, and sorcery, just the practices which the narrative of Kings connects so prominently with Manasseh's reign.

The code does not, however, confine itself to matters of worship and its purification. It is permeated throughout with the moral conception of God and of human obligation which the prophets had made paramount in their teaching. It does not suggest, as they did, an antithesis between worship and righteousness, but contemplates a spirit of justice and mercy in worship as well as other departments of human activity. The slave, sojourner, fatherless, and widow shall share in the joyous harvest festivals with the freeman and his

family. Lost property shall be carefully guarded
for its owner; building law provides against un-
necessary accident; the hired servant is to be paid
promptly; bribery and injustice to the defenseless
are forbidden; a general tax for the support of the
poor is imposed upon the fruit of the land.

That noble decalogue which we commonly style
the Ten Commandments probably assumed the
familiar form in which it appears in Exodus
20:1–17 at about the time of which we are now
speaking. In contrast with the earlier codes of
chapters 34 and 20:22—23:19, it shows the controlling interest of eighth-century prophecy, making
moral requirements more prominent than ritual.
It has not yet crystallized into absolutely fixed
form, for in Deuteronomy chapter 5, it appears in
slightly different form, the most notable variation
being in the humanitarian ground there urged for
the observance of the Sabbath.

In Deuteronomy the Decalogue serves to introduce a long address which is itself introductory to
the great code we have been discussing. The
address as a whole insists above all else upon the
unity of Yahweh and his supremacy in heaven and
earth, and upon his justice and his mercy manifested toward Israel in her past history. On
Yahweh's character and on his love for Israel is
based the exhortation to obey the great laws that
follow.

Previous codes had been brief and often fragmentary guides for conduct, but in this new lawbook the effort is made to offer a complete guide for the daily life of the Hebrew, based on the best thought and practice of both the priests and the prophets.

It was probably while Manasseh still reigned, when the purer practice of the Jerusalem temple was being confused by the introduction of foreign cults, and when the voice of true prophecy was stopped by force, that men who shared the human longing for ritual which the prophets had flouted, and who combined with this the prophets' insight into the truly ethical character of God, compiled the great law code of Deuteronomy and prefixed to this the great hortatory address of chapters 5–11.

This work marked a new stage of thought in Israel's religious development, nothing less than regulating the entire life of the individual by divinely sanctioned law.

The occasion was not favorable for the publication of such a book, the existence of which, for the time, it was necessary to keep quite secret. Apparently it was laid away somewhere about the temple, while the conditions fostered by Manasseh continued to prevail during the brief reign of his son and the opening years of his grandson's rule. Then the voice of true prophecy was once more permitted in public; Zephaniah and Jeremiah began to condemn existing conditions in unsparing terms.

By this time there had come to be complete skepticism on the part of some who denied that Yahweh acted at all, either for good or for ill; but the young king, who had now reached manhood, was, in some way, moved to act for the repair of the dilapidated temple. In the course of the work undertaken the law-book composed some years before was brought to light. Whether its compilers were still living we do not know, but now at length the time was favorable for their book to be adopted as the authoritative law of the land. The reforms carried out by the young and ardent Josiah, as described in the Books of Kings, were just those contemplated by the law of Deuteronomy so far as this law could be applied by royal action.

The idolatrous priests and altars, vessels, and symbols, that were in Jerusalem and Judea, even the altars of Yahweh in Judea and in the territory that once pertained to Northern Israel, were defiled, so that worship might be strictly limited to the Jerusalem temple, as the new law rigidly ordained. Such provisions for enforcing the outward forms of religion were open to legal enforcement; the inner spirit of the law and its application to individual relations were quite another matter. Nevertheless, now for the first time, the nation

was outwardly recognizing Yahweh alone throughout all its borders, and was worshiping him with
rites that were freed from the cruel and debasing
practices characteristic of the baalism of Canaan.
The agricultural feasts and other elements of ritual
learned from the Canaanites were now at last a part
of the worship of the austere God of the desert,
but freed from their old excesses of wine and prosti-
tution they were transformed into harmony with
the character of the God who demanded control
of the bodily propensities, but had now come to be
officially recognized as the giver of the corn and
wine of fruitful Canaan.

We regarded it as one of the most notable steps
in the progress of Hebrew religious thought when
the God of Sinai was conceived as dominant in
Canaan too. We counted it an even greater
advance step when Amos clearly recognized that
the God of Israel was really the God of nations,
shaping history according to just purposes. It
is a hardly less notable step in progress when
we find that the worship of this God has been
able to take into itself the old nature-worship of
Canaan and to retain its elements of beauty and
truth, while so largely removing its less worthy
elements.

While Josiah lived this ideal condition in the
outward form of religion was no doubt maintained.
The king was supported in his exclusive recognition

of Yahweh by the prosperity which his people now enjoyed. Assyria, the ancient oppressor, was tottering to her ruin, and, for the time, no other nation interfered to prevent Josiah from extending his rule over the territory of Northern Israel; the mixed population settled there by the Assyrians a century before had already sought to learn the worship of Yahweh as that of the god of the land (II Kings 17:24–33).

Assyria's weakness proved, however, the opportunity of Egypt, whose king determined to annex all Syria, including Palestine. Seeking to stay this step, Josiah met his death fighting bravely in defense of his country's independence. Under Egyptian suzerainty Josiah's unworthy son followed in the vassal steps of his great-grandfather, Manasseh, and reintroduced a great variety of foreign cults. Ezekiel, in 8:9–18, gives vivid pictures of the temple practices as he had known them at about this time.

Like many another promising reform undertaken since, the effects of that of Josiah and the law of Deuteronomy were quickly swept away by the returning surge of all that had been eradicated with such great effort. Despite the shock of the defeat and death of Josiah, who had seemed almost the complete fulfilment of the hope of an ideal ruler on the throne of his ancestor David, the prophetic party was strong enough to place upon the throne a son **of** Josiah who was in sympathy with the reform, but Pharaoh Necho, returning from the conquest **of** Northern Syria, took this prince in bonds to Egypt and put in his place one who accepted complacently all foreign innovation.

Nevertheless, ground had been gained that could not be wholly and permanently lost. It was much that, for twelve or fifteen years, a law requiring such pure religious and ethical practices had been the actual standard of the state. Henceforth it will be an ideal standard for many, and though the superstitious practices that Deuteronomy had condemned come sweeping back for a time, they are doomed to disappear from among the Jewish people and to be replaced by a type of worship as pure as that demanded by this code.

It is true that reform by law alone cannot deal with the roots of conduct and that such reform, by royal or other external authority, cannot last when that authority is changed or weakened; yet moral and spiritual advances which do not take shape in institutions and laws are likely to remain intangible and evanescent. The Book of Deuteronomy was a most remarkable attempt to formulate new moral and spiritual ideals into a tangible social order intelligible to the ordinary man. It was a most remarkable effort also to use all that was worthy in the existing state and religious order for the realization of a social and religious life that should make possible for the people as a whole the ideals of the prophets which, as yet, only the select few had been able to apprehend.

SUPPLEMENTARY READING

Peake, *The Religion of Israel*, pp. 82-88.
Addis, *Hebrew Religion*, pp. 181-97.
Ottley, *The Religion of Israel*, pp. 91-101.
Budde, *Religion of Israel to the Exile*, pp. 160-80.
H. P. Smith, *The Religion of Israel*, pp. 179-95.
Peters, *The Religion of the Hebrews*, pp. 242-66.
Marti, *Religion of the Old Testament*, pp. 184-89.

CHAPTER VIII

THE DISCOVERY OF THE INDIVIDUAL

References for study—
- (1) Jer. 11:1–8.
- (2) Jer. 7:1–20.
- (3) Jer. 11:18–23; 16:1–9; 18:18; 20:1–2; 37:11–21; 38:1–13; 44:1–2, 7–10, 15–19.
- (4) Jer. 12:1–6; 15:10–11, 15–21; 18:19–23.
- (5) Jer. 31:29–34; Ezek., chap. 18; 33:1–9.
- (6) II Kings 25:1–12.
- (7) Ezek., chaps. 1, 8; 11:22–25.

Note in (1) Jeremiah's itinerating mission; in (2) the false and true grounds of national confidence; in (3) Jeremiah's isolation and sufferings; in (4) his personal intercourse with God; in (5) the relation between God and the individual; in (6) the fall of the nation; in (7) Ezekiel's vision of God and of the idolatry in the temple.

The recorded sermons of Jeremiah connect themselves with the five years preceding Josiah's reform and the years following the king's death. The narrative concerning Jeremiah's preaching, in the cities of Judah and the streets of Jerusalem, the words of the covenant commanded the fathers in the day that they were brought out of the land of Egypt, suggests that he participated in Josiah's reform, carrying the message of Deuteronomy directly to the people. If this was the case, he did

not care to preserve the addresses of this era when
he committed the substance of his earlier preaching
to writing.

Jeremiah's early preaching must have helped
to prepare the way for the reform of Josiah. How
large a part he actually took in the measures of
reform which the king carried out we do not know.
He lived through the years of outward conformity
to the high and exacting standards of Deuteronomy
and, when the old evils came back under the reign
of Jehoiakim, he promptly faced the crisis, warning
king and people of the coming downfall of the state.

A century before, in the face of Assyrian attack,
Isaiah had assured his contemporaries that Jerusalem would not be captured. The sudden withdrawal of the Assyrian army had vindicated his
prediction, and so it had now grown into a dogma
of faith that Yahweh's city could not be conquered.
Jeremiah found the people confident that although
they might steal, murder, commit adultery, swear
falsely, and follow other gods, if they only came
and stood before Yahweh in his house they would
escape judgment upon their sins. This type of
faith nullified the teachings of Isaiah and the
requirements of Deuteronomy, yet it was based on
Isaiah's own words. That which was temporary,
true for the particular occasion to which Isaiah was
addressing himself, had been erected into a universal doctrine, absolutely hostile to Isaiah's own

deep teachings of God's moral demands upon the nation.

From the death of Josiah to the complete destruction of Jerusalem by the Babylonians in 586 B.C., Jeremiah saw the coming doom and sought to avert it by leading the people to bend to the storm of Babylonian conquest and to amend their moral conduct so as to secure healthy internal conditions in their little state. His clear foresight that Babylon was destined to supersede Egypt in the control of Palestine, and that Jerusalem must fall if she persisted in her chosen course, made him seem a traitor, for he opposed the policy of the government and tried to weaken the people's purpose to resist Babylon.

Jeremiah was a man of peculiarly sensitive temperament, akin in thought and spirit to Hosea rather than to the stern Amos or the majestic Isaiah. At the outset of his ministry it was clear that he never could welcome the duties of a great prophet; nothing but an unrelenting sense that he had been chosen for a hard task could urge him to his mission. His was a nature that longed for fellowship and sympathy, yet his work separated him absolutely from human companionship and support, and brought upon him cruel misunderstanding and persecution.

The men of his own town, Anathoth, plotted against his life, so that he felt himself, in his ignorance of their purpose, like a gentle lamb that is led to the slaughter. Realizing that children, mothers, and fathers must die a grievous death in the ruin that was drawing near, he felt that he must not take a wife and beget sons and daughters to share the approaching misery. As the bearer of the message that God had taken away his peace from the people, he could not enter into the house of mourning to comfort nor into the house of feasting to share joy. Although he was of honorable priestly family, the priest who was chief officer of the temple put him into the stocks like a common criminal. Falsely accused of attempting to desert to the Babylonians, he was beaten and thrown into prison. Finally he was lowered into a miry pit in the court of the guard, where he was left to die by the princes, and was rescued only by the intercession of a servant of the king who chanced to hear of his fate.

After the capture of Jerusalem, Jeremiah was permitted to remain in Palestine with a little community of the people who were not removed with the exiles to Babylon. A little later the governor of this community was murdered and, against the advice of Jeremiah, the people fled to Egypt, taking him with them. Our last glimpse of the faithful prophet shows him warning his fellow-countrymen in that land and flouted by them with specious argument.

The outward vicissitudes of Jeremiah's life were sufficient to give his story deep pathos. The inner sufferings of such a shrinking, tender nature, forced into isolation, misunderstood and rejected, seeing his loved nation despise his clear prevision and plunge on to destruction, make his biography one of the tragedies of history. And yet it was just this suffering and loneliness that forced him along the path of consolation and triumph.

Jeremiah's words reveal to us the inner life of the prophet as do those of none of his predecessors. We have seen Elijah feeling that he alone was faithful to the God of Israel, journeying to the ancient mountain of the presence there to gain new strength and guidance from the still small voice; but Jeremiah shows us again and again how he turned in perplexity and rebellion to the unseen presence. He reasoned his cause with God. Instead of a solution of his questions or an answer to his cry "How long?" he received assurance that a far harder course was before him; he had been running with the footmen, but he must contend against horses. With such assurance he went out strong to meet his duty. Crying woe that he had been born to be a man of strife, he received promise of victory.

His every difficulty he carried to the one whom Hosea's words had taught him to count Israel's loving husband and father. In this experience he is led far beyond that which Hosea had seen. To the earlier prophet Yahweh was revealed as the husband and father of the nation; but Jeremiah learned, in his isolation from men and his communion with God, that the individual may stand before God, apart from his nation.

Not only on the side of personal communion with God, resulting in strength and guidance for his own personal life, did Jeremiah come to know God's relation to the individual; he applied the doctrine to the divine judgments as well. Deuteronomy had promised the nation permanence and prosperity in the land if it would keep Yahweh's statutes and serve him only and had threatened corresponding judgments upon the nation if it were faithless. When troubles clouded thick upon the nation, the people were evidently prone to count these as judgments for the sins of their fathers. "The fathers have eaten sour grapes and the children's teeth are set on edge" seems to have been their favorite proverb. Jeremiah looked forward to the day when this convenient shifting of responsibility should have passed away with the recognition of the truth that God deals with each according to his own deserts: "Every man that eateth the sour grapes, his teeth shall be set on edge; every one shall die for his own iniquity."

Jeremiah just glimpses this aspect of truth, but Ezekiel, preaching as a captive in Babylon before the destruction of Jerusalem, catches up the thought and works it out after his thorough manner.

He asserts that the soul of each is God's, whether father or son, and declares: "The soul that sinneth, it shall die." This he exemplifies at length in the case of a righteous father and wicked son who may not be spared because of his father's virtue, and then carries out his illustration by assuming that this one's son does not follow in the evil steps of his father. He even asserts that the individual is not condemned on his own past record, but on his present conduct, and declares that the Lord has no pleasure in the death of the wicked.

Ezekiel applies his doctrine of individual responsibility as an appeal to others to turn from their wickedness and live, but he does not fail to apply it in full measure to himself. If he as the city's watchman fails to warn of the approach of danger, the blood of the city is upon his head; if he gives warning, then their blood is upon the heads of those who have not heeded. Thus thoroughly does Ezekiel carry out the personal responsibility side of Jeremiah's doctrine of individualism.

It is difficult for those who live in a land and age of highly developed individualism to realize the nature of tribal or communal consciousness which always marks earlier stages of development. In these earlier stages one hardly thinks of himself as having more of an individual life, apart from the clan or tribe, than we think of the cell as having individual life distinct from the organism of which it is a part. In studying any phase of the development of civilization we must learn to interpret early phenomena from the standpoint of tribal consciousness. It is an indication of comparatively late and mature development when this yields to definitely personal consciousness in which the separate man, woman, or child is thought of as an end apart from the group. In Israel, the years that mark the downfall of the state show the most clearly marked stage of this great and fateful transition.

In the early years of struggle for the land common loyalty to the covenant God was the one force which was able to change the tribal consciousness of early Israel into something like a national consciousness. When the remnant of the divided nation was facing extinction more than four centuries later, it was the loyalty of the prophet Jeremiah to the nation and its deserted God which led him to such an experience of his own standing with God that he found the individual whose fellowship with his God might exist, though the nation proved faithless, and whose life as a separate reality, dear to God, might continue though the nation fell and its members were scattered abroad.

The people who superstitiously conceived the divine presence in the temple as a palladium of the nation's safety dwelt upon the level of the peoples about them, who thought of each god as belonging to a particular district or group. When their nation, city, and temple should fall and they themselves be scattered to distant regions, they might be expected to count their god as overthrown and to seek the favor of the deities in whose lands they found themselves. Under the tribal or national conception of Deity the scattering of the nation might easily mean the obliteration of the name of Yahweh from the face of the earth, as the name of many another god has been lost in the destruction of the people who acknowledged him.

While Jeremiah struggled against such catastrophe in Jerusalem, Ezekiel worked to the same end among the exiles in Babylonia. The largest band of those deported from Jerusalem to Babylonia was the company taken in the year 597, when the city and temple escaped destruction for the time. Among those taken at this time was the young priest Ezekiel. Five years later, on the banks of one of Babylon's canal-rivers, near the ancient city of Nippur, he had a vision of Yahweh coming, seated on a throne borne by strange, composite creatures, similar to those the prophet had seen sculptured at the entrances of palaces and temples in the land of his captivity.

Whatever may have been the meaning of all the symbolism of this vision, it showed three things: (1) the God of Israel superior to the mythical beings reverenced by Israel's conquerors; (2) this God a mobile being, not limited to one place; (3) this God present in ancient and mighty Babylon itself. In vivid picture Ezekiel described to his fellow-exiles, who still trusted Yahweh speedily to restore them to his city, the idolatrous practices which forced their God to leave his polluted temple. At last he described Yahweh as rising from his temple and leaving it to its fate. By such pictorial teaching he sought to free men from the idea that the fall of Jerusalem meant the defeat of Yahweh, no longer able to maintain his abode against the attack of Marduk, god of Babylon.

When Jerusalem fell in the year 586, after its mad rebellion and stubborn resistance, and other thousands were deported to Babylon, and still others fled to Egypt, the people who had based false hopes on the temple as their assurance of safety were in despair; but some must have remembered that Ezekiel had predicted this doom and had taught them to think of their God as having voluntarily left his temple and suffered its destruction. Now they turned to the prophet whose prediction had been vindicated. Suddenly his message changed from one of doom to one of hope of restoration. His task was a discouraging one, yet his faith burned bright and the exiles in Babylon did not all give up faith; they became, indeed, the hope of a restored and purified Judah.

Thus, in the fall of the nation, Ezekiel taught the exiles to recognize their individual responsibility and standing before God, regardless of their fathers' failures or virtues, regardless even of their own past errors. He promised them, too, a heart of flesh in place of their stony heart.

Jeremiah, who in Jerusalem had preached immediate doom and later restoration, had seen more deeply than Ezekiel into the only condition which could make restoration worth while. Ezekiel was probably too young to remember the reform of Josiah through which Jeremiah had lived. The older prophet had seen the inadequacy of the most perfectly formulated contract to secure permanently a pure national life. He had seen the superficial and temporary character of reform by royal authority and had learned that only the law written in the heart could be adequate—that only the people that knew God from the least of them even unto the greatest of them could be truly his people.

Jeremiah contrasted thus the new covenant with the old, which had been so perfectly formulated in the Book of Deuteronomy and so faithfully tried by the good King Josiah: "Behold the days come, saith Jehovah, that I will make a new covenant with the house of Israel, and with the house of Judah: not according to the covenant that I made with their fathers in the day that I took them by the hand to bring them out of the land of Egypt;

which my covenant they brake, although I was a husband unto them, saith Jehovah.

"But this is the covenant that I will make with the house of Israel after those days, saith Jehovah: I will put my law in their inward parts, and in their heart will I write it; and I will be their God, and they shall be my people: and they shall teach no more every man his neighbor, and every man his brother, saying, Know Jehovah; for they shall all know me, from the least of them unto the greatest of them, saith Jehovah: for I will forgive their iniquity, and their sin will I remember no more."

This conception of the new covenant is one of the loftiest heights reached in the religion of Israel. It was far beyond the apprehension of the mass of the people, even of their religious teachers, but it was one of the most vital statements of religious truth that has ever been formulated. It meant the possibility of transition from a limited, national religion to an individual and so universal religion.

SUPPLEMENTARY READING

Peake, *The Religion of Israel*, pp. 89–102.
Addis, *Hebrew Religion*, pp. 197–206.
Ottley, *The Religion of Israel*, pp. 101–5, 116.
Budde, *Religion of Israel to the Exile*, pp. 181–99.
H. P. Smith, *The Religion of Israel*, pp. 162–78.
Peters, *The Religion of the Hebrews*, pp. 267–82.
Badè, *The Old Testament in the Light of To-Day*, pp. 258–80.

CHAPTER IX

TWO IDEALS FROM THE EXILE

References for study—

(1) Ezek. 37:15–28.

(2) Ezek. 43:1–5; chap. 44.

(3) Lev., chap. 23; Exod. 34:18–26.

(4) Isa. 40:12–26; 42:5–6; 45:12, 18, 20–25; 46:1–11; 44:6–20.

(5) Isa. 55:6–9; 58:5–12; 61:1–3.

(6) Isa. 42:1–4, 7, 18–22; 43:10; 44:1–5, 21; 48:20; 49:1–7; 52:13—53:12.

Note in (1) Ezekiel's promised covenant in contrast to Jeremiah's; in (2) the return of God to his restored temple and provisions for the ritual purity of temple and priesthood; in (3) the laws of the feasts in the Levitical code in comparison with those of the early Judean code; in (4) the power of Yahweh in contrast to the gods of Babylon; in (5) the true character and purposes of Yahweh; in (6) the characteristics and experiences of the Servant.

Ezekiel, like Jeremiah, looked forward to a covenant made with the restored nation, but he failed to see that this covenant needed to be of an essentially different nature from the old one. His idea was that God by his power would multiply his people, setting his sanctuary in their midst, and that the nations would be forced to recognize his presence there. While Ezekiel was a prophet with some recognition of the inner conditions of life, he was much more a priest, concerned with the external and visible institutions that express the relations of the people with their God.

It was near the close of his ministry, in the twenty-fifth year of his captivity, that Ezekiel saw in detailed vision the restoration of the temple, city, and land, with more magnificent provision for sacrificial worship than had ever been realized while the kingdom stood. The vision occupies the last nine chapters of Ezekiel's book; of these the first three describe the ideal temple, and especially its surrounding courts and gates. Next comes a description of God's returning to his restored house, the sequel to the vision which the prophet had seen, nearly twenty years before, of God's departure from his temple.

Mindful of the pollution which had driven the Holy One from his ancient temple, Ezekiel prescribed elaborate safeguards for the sanctity of the house to be built. No foreigner was to enter the sacred precincts, and those members of the tribe of Levi who had formerly officiated at the high places were to be permitted only the more menial duties in connection with the temple and its sacrifices. The truly priestly functions were to be limited to those Levites who had officiated in Solomon's temple. These were counted sons of Zadok, who was priest in the days of David and

Solomon, and whose ancestry was traced back to Aaron.

The Deuteronomic law had provided for the Levites of the devastated high places equal rights with the Jerusalem priests, but Ezekiel's ideas of the purity of the temple revolted at this and introduced the sharp distinction between the priests and the other Levites characteristic of later Judaism. How far Ezekiel's other careful provisions for the physical purity of the priests were the mere writing down of ancient practices and how far they were new ideas of his we cannot always be sure; certainly the pre-exilic codes which are preserved make no such elaborate provisions for ritual cleanness. The judicial functions which he ascribed to the priests were such as had long been their prerogatives.

Detailed provisions were made as to the various kinds of offerings; and a mechanically ideal allotment of the land to the Twelve Tribes, quite different from their historical apportionment, is described at length. According to this ideal, there were to be seven tribes north and five south of the city and sanctuary, each tribe owning a strip from the sea to the desert. About the sanctuary the separate domains of the priests, the Levites, and the prince were arranged.

Ezekiel, as a young man of priestly family and ardent devotion to his God, had seen the mixed

mass of foreign cults practiced in the temple during
the years of reaction, after Josiah's death. He
must have realized through those bitter years that
the centralization of worship in Jerusalem, insisted
upon in the law of Deuteronomy, had not accomplished its purpose in securing the exclusive worship
of the God of Israel. Now, in the latter years of his
life, he planned for the future an arrangement of
the restored community which it seemed must
protect the sanctuary for its own God. He was
filled with a sense of Yahweh's holiness, but this
seems to have been in his mind more ceremonial
than moral. He had something of the ethical
conception of God that his great predecessors had
developed during some centuries of upward progress, but the original idea of holiness, separation,
was more prominent in his thought.

Other men of priestly mind and inheritance, in
the early years of exile, formulated a code of
ritual law in which the word "holiness" is so often
repeated that it is known as the "Holiness Code."
This body of law was taken up into the later Book
of Leviticus, of which it now forms chapters 17–26.
The laws deal mainly with ceremonial purity,
qualifications for the priesthood, religious festivals,
and kindred themes. A comparison of the direc-
tions for the great annual feasts with those found
in our earliest ritual code may serve at once to
indicate the continuity of Israel's ritual and the

gradual elaboration of the laws which prescribe its practices.

Probably the Holiness Code did little more, in most matters with which it dealt, than formulate the practices of the true worship of Yahweh as they were understood in the Jerusalem temple before its destruction. So long as the temple stood and its worship was conducted by a succession of trained priests, very little was needed by way of written law to direct its forms of worship; the fall of the temple and the transporting of its priests to a distant land seem to have brought about very speedily a certain amount of literary activity on the part of these priests. We shall find this activity increasing among the Jewish priests of Babylon in subsequent generations.

The first ideal of Israel's religion which we find assuming fixed and permanent form in the exile is that of rigid provision for guarding the holiness of Yahweh and his people, by the preservation of those rites which were now counted his true and time-honored worship, and by the establishment of new rules which should prevent such admixture of foreign worship as had characterized the last years of Solomon's temple.

All this involved a turning away from the ideas of the prophets and an emphasis upon ritual law such as not even Deuteronomy had contemplated. Had it been simply a temporary reaction against the prophetic interpretation of religion, it would not have demanded prolonged discussion; it was rather a momentous point in the age-long struggle between the prophetic and the priestly sides of Israel's religion, indicating the dominance of priestly ideals for ages to come.

The work of Ezekiel and of the codifiers of the Holiness Code belongs to the earlier years of exile. Toward the latter end of this period stirring events among the nations called forth once more the spirit of true prophecy. For some years we continue to hear a most wonderful chorus of prophetic voices that has sung itself on through the ages as the expression of the highest hope and faith of which the human spirit is capable. Later editors affixed these songs to the Book of Isaiah's prophecies, whence they are often styled the Second Isaiah.

The rise of Cyrus, who established the Medo-Persian Empire and extended it westward to the Aegean, seems to have assured an enlightened seer in Babylon that deliverance for the exiles was near at hand. The power of their rulers had so far crushed the hope of his people that they had little confidence in the purpose or ability of their God to deliver them. To meet this situation the new poet-prophet gave expression to the loftiest descriptions of Yahweh's universal power that had yet been spoken. Isaiah had heard him acclaimed as the one whose glory filled the whole earth and had thought of him as shaping the course of the great nations to his will; but the unnamed prophet of the exile knows him as the one that "created the heavens and stretched them forth, that spread abroad the earth and that which cometh out of it, that giveth breath unto the people upon it and spirit to them that walk therein." He represents Yahweh as declaring, "I have made the earth and created man upon it; I even my hands have stretched out the heavens, and all their host have I commanded."

In these oracles we have at last reached the expression of unequivocal monotheism. The great prophets of the eighth century came close to this in their realization that their God directed the movements of the nations, but it required the experiences of exile, the widened view of the world below and the starry heavens above, such as came after years of life amid the culture of ancient Babylonia, to bring to conscious expression the definite doctrine of God as the creator of all things.

The last king of Babylon, under whose rule this great monotheistic prophet lived, was a most devoted worshiper of the ancient gods of his land, divinities which had been honored centuries before the ancestors of Israel covenanted with Yahweh at Sinai. Their fame had spread so far that the name of one of them, the moon-god Sin, was borne by the mountain where Moses first met Yahweh, and the mountain whence he viewed the promised land, Nebo, bore the name of another of these ancient gods. Now the Babylonian king, whose name, Nabonidus, means "Nebo elevated," was trusting these deities of ancient, widespread recognition to protect his land and theirs from the rising power of the upstart Cyrus. In Babylon, Nabonidus repaired the ancient temples and brought the gods of the other cities in stately procession to his capital to assure its safety.

The captive prophet had apparently seen such processions of helpless images and was moved with scorn: "Bel boweth down, Nebo stoopeth; their idols are upon the beasts, and upon the cattle," he cries out. The excavations of the past few years have uncovered the stately procession street leading up to the great temple of Babylon, a street whose walled sides were covered with blue glazed tile, bearing tawny lions in bas-relief, that seem almost alive through the splendid artistry of the ancient ceramists; hence today we can picture more vividly than would have been possible for us five years ago the idol-processions that called forth the scorn of our prophet of the sixth century before Christ. Again and again the prophet heaps scorn upon those who make and honor images, and never more effectively than in chapter 44, where he pictures the carpenter as warming himself with part of the tree that he has felled, kindling part to bake bread, and making a god of the residue.

In his exultant sense of the unique power of Yahweh this prophet does not wholly lose sight of the moral nature which to Amos was the very essence of divinity: "He has formed the earth to be inhabited and speaks righteousness; he is a just God; looking unto him all the ends of the earth may be saved." It is, however, in the oracles delivered a few years later, after Cyrus' capture of Babylon, and perhaps by another poet, that the full moral quality seen by Hosea and Jeremiah is ascribed to this God, now apprehended as universal Creator and Preserver. In chapters 55, 58, and 61 we find God described as one who will have mercy and abundantly pardon the wicked who forsakes his way; one who would not have the fast one of sackcloth and ashes, but of letting the oppressed go free, dealing bread to the hungry, and covering the naked; one who anoints his representative to preach good tidings to the poor, to proclaim liberty to the captives, and to comfort all who mourn.

In this group of oracles that reflect the last days of exile and perhaps the early years of restoration in Jerusalem, the progressive revelation of God through the prophets of ancient Israel reaches heights that seem final. Jesus of Nazareth, moving among men in bodily form, will make this con-

ception of God tangible, fuller, too, in the details of
its meaning for human life, but even he can scarcely
give man a loftier conception of the power and
nature of God than that embodied in these oracles
of the sixth century before his incarnation, except
in one profound aspect. That aspect is glimpsed
at least in the passages concerning Yahweh's servant which are found within these groups of oracles.

The principal servant-passages may be parts
of what was originally a single poem that have been
separated as they were inwoven with the other
songs of chapters 40–55, or they may have been
independent oracles with a common theme. At
any rate there seems to be a progress in the interpretation of the servant from the point when the
figure first meets us in chapter 44 to its final
appearance in chapter 53.

At the beginning the identity of the servant
upon whom Yahweh has put his spirit is not made
clear, though his lofty mission of establishing
justice in the earth and bringing the prisoners out
of the dungeon is stated, and we are told that he
is to do this without breaking a bruised reed or
quenching a dimly burning wick. Later in the
same chapter the title "Yahweh's servant" seems
to be applied to his people, who are, however,
characterized as deaf and blind. In the following
chapter the scattered people of Israel, though
blind, are God's witnesses and servant, and in the

next Israel is definitely addressed as "my servant" more than once, and the title is again applied
to the people in chapter 48 as redeemed from
the captivity of Babylon.

In chapter 49 the servant is addressed as Israel,
but his function now is to bring Jacob or Israel
back to his God, to raise up the tribes of Jacob, and
to restore the preserved of Israel. He is also to
be a light to the Gentiles and to be Yahweh's salvation unto the ends of the earth. Although
addressed as Israel, the servant here cannot be
more than the faithful part of the people whose
mission is to bring back the unfaithful and to
spread the light to the world.

In the great final passage (52:13—53:12) the
figure seems individualized as that of one who has
for the sake of others borne cruel punishment,
pouring out his soul unto death, so that it has been
made an offering for sin.

Whoever is in the mind of the ancient prophet-
poet, whether it is suffering Israel personified, or,
better, the loyal portion of Israel which has borne
the sins of the nation in anguish of soul, or whether
it is an individual, past or future, the picture suddenly opens to us fleeting, baffling vistas into the
universal truth of life. The supreme servants of
God who have greatly served mankind have ever
been despised and rejected of men, men of sorrows
and acquainted with grief, bearing the iniquities

of many. Hosea and Jeremiah come to mind among those who had already lived and died when the poem of the Suffering Servant was written. The martyrs of religion, and of every other high devotion, men who have greatly risen above the level of their own age, have drawn others up toward their high vision only as they themselves have borne the iniquities. The humble servants of God, whose loving devotion has sought to win the base or the unseeing near them to a true life, have just as really exemplified the great law of life which the ancient poet saw.

Jesus of Nazareth, who most fully and perfectly realized the mission of the Servant of God, counted himself the Son sent in self-sacrificing love by the Father whose heart yearned over all his children on earth. He taught us to see that God himself is the supreme example of this universal law of life. Thus in these oracles the truth is glimpsed; five hundred years later it will be made clear and will complete Israel's revelation of God, the truth that the just and holy Creator, the one God, is self-sacrificing love.

From the exile come two strangely contrasting ideals of loyalty to God. One is that of uttermost loyalty manifest in formal worship, to be given to him alone, by his exclusive people, who are to be guarded from all foreign contamination. The other is loyalty manifested in another kind of sacrifice, not the offering of bulls and goats, but a life of self-sacrifice for service, if need be unto the death, not jealously guarded from contamination but a light unto the Gentiles. In the vicissitudes of the generations immediately to follow the former will prove the path by which the restored community will preserve its integrity and its faith. Five centuries must pass before the other is adopted as the center and heart of true religion.

SUPPLEMENTARY READING

Peake, *The Religion of Israel*, pp. 103–24.
Addis, *Hebrew Religion*, pp. 207–53.
Ottley, *The Religion of Israel*, pp. 106–26.
Budde, *Religion of Israel to the Exile*, pp. 199–218.
H. P. Smith, *The Religion of Israel*, pp. 196–210, 250–62.
Peters, *The Religion of the Hebrews*, pp. 283–315, 321–26.
Marti, *Religion of the Old Testament*, pp. 174–83, 189–90.

CHAPTER X

LEGALISM TRIUMPHANT

References for study—

    (1) Ezra 5:1–3; 6:14–15; Hag. 1—2:9; Zech. 1:7–17.

    (2) Mal. 1:6–14; 2:10–17.

    (3) Neh. 1:1–3; 2:1–8; 6:15; chap. 13.

    (4) Neh. 8:1–3, 9; 9:1–4, 32–38; 10:28–37.

    (5) Gen. 2:1–3; 9:3–4, 8–12; 17:1–4, 10–13.

    (6) Lev., chaps. 1, 16.

Note in (1) the facts as to the rebuilding of the temple; in (2) indifference, skepticism, and foreign intermarriage about sixty years after the rebuilding of the temple; in (3) the conditions that Nehemiah found and the specific reforms that he carried out; in (4) the priestly reforms attributed to Ezra; in (5) religious institutions conceived as pre-Mosaic; in (6) elaborateness of detail in priestly organization and ritual.

In the year 520 B.C. a prophet, Haggai, roused the people of Jerusalem to undertake the rebuilding of their temple, which had lain in ruins since the destruction of Jerusalem in 586.

Eighteen years had passed since Cyrus captured Babylon and applied to the deported peoples whom he found there the liberal and clement policy of allowing them to re-establish their national worships in their own lands. Very few of the Jewish

139

exiles had as yet ventured the long and hard journey back to Judea and the more difficult renewal of life in their devastated land. Zerubbabel, the prince of the royal line, had come back as local governor, and Joshua, of the line of Aaron, as priest. With them had come, no doubt, some little company, but it is to the people of the land rather than to returned exiles that Haggai addresses himself. Already homes have been built amid the ruins of the city, but neither city wall nor temple has been restored.

Soon Zechariah adds his appeal to that of Haggai. With symbolic visions that recall those of Ezekiel he supplements the plain and stirring speech of the other.

The resources of the community were as nothing in comparsion with those which Solomon had had at his disposal four hundred and fifty years before. Doubtless the old stone still lay in confusion about the temple mount near at hand. The timber portions of the ancient structure had, however, been destroyed by fire when Nebuchadrezzar laid the city waste. The builders soon grew discouraged as they saw how imperfect a restoration of the old temple it would be possible for them to make. Ezekiel had pictured the former temple rebuilt and surrounded with courts on a much more elaborate scale than those about Solomon's temple. The reality proved a sad contrast to the remembered

glory of the former structures and to the glowing
hope of Ezekiel.   Yet the people labored on and
in four years completed their work.   With all the
resources of the united kingdom of Israel and the
co-operation of the king of Tyre, Solomon's temple
had required seven years for its building.

The sacrificial ritual of the new temple must
have fallen as far short of Ezekiel's ardent vision
as the building itself.   The prophet Malachi gives
a scathing picture of the worship of the people
a little later.   Haggai had promised that the precious things of all nations would come to fill the
house with glory; Zechariah had assured them that
the sin of the nation had been expiated in the exile
and that now the divine grace would perpetually
supply the lamp of the temple through the anointed
prince and priest.   The years since the completion
of the temple have dragged for a half-century and
more; Jerusalem has remained thinly populated,
unwalled, and unprotected, the byword of petty
neighboring peoples once subject to its rule.   The
great mass of the descendants of the exiles have
found it more comfortable to remain in Babylonia,
where many of them have gained success in the
commercial life of that wealthy portion of the
Persian Empire.

Malachi finds the discouraged little community
of Jerusalem sure that evildoers are blessed of God,
or asking scornfully, Where is the God of justice?

They maintain, it is true, the semblance of worship at the temple, bringing to the altar their blind, lame, and sick animals, such as they would never dare offer as tribute to their governor. Instead of carrying out Ezekiel's ideals of rigid exclusion of all foreigners from the temple, the people of the Jerusalem community have found it advantageous to intermarry with the daughters of their pagan neighbors, even divorcing their Jewish wives in order to make these alliances.

The picture is a disheartening one, and when news of these conditions reaches a Jew of the east who has risen to high and favored position in the household of the Persian monarch, he is stirred to the depths of his nature. This truly great man, Nehemiah, has told us in a beautiful little memoir how he obtained permission of Artaxerxes to visit Palestine, with authority, as governor, to rebuild the city walls and received a requisition on the keeper of the king's forest for the timber needed.

It was quite impossible for the little community centering in Jerusalem to keep itself free from foreign intermixture and to observe fully its distinctive religious practices while the city lay open for all who wished to enter. Under the able leadership of Nehemiah, who proved a most efficient organizer of the workers, the walls were erected in a surprisingly brief time. The jealous neighboring peoples looked with deep anxiety upon the

efforts which might make Jerusalem once more
the military and political capital of all Palestine.
Their plots to get possession of Nehemiah or to
discredit him in the eyes of his fellow-countrymen
were very shrewdly conceived, but one who had
risen to a position of trust at the court of an oriental
empire, though he was singularly simple-hearted
and direct by nature, had learned how to deal with
all kinds of conspiracy.

When the walls were completed and gates set
up that could be opened and closed at will, it
became possible to enforce Sabbath cessation of
trade, even excluding the foreign fish peddlers who
had been wont to come on that day. Sabbath
rest had been a marked characteristic of Hebrew
religious observance in pre-exilic days; the codes
from the earliest of Exodus, chapter 34, to Deuteronomy had all made provision for the day of rest.
In the time of Amos the merchants observed the
new moons and Sabbaths with cessation of selling,
however eager they might be to get back to their
dishonest trade.

During the exile, when the sacrifices that
Deuteronomy had limited to the Jerusalem temple
ceased, the Sabbath could still be observed in
Babylonia. From the exile onward this day
became, among the orthodox Jews, a more and
more prominent and cherished institution. But the
degenerate Judeans of Nehemiah's time apparently

cared little for its sanctity; when the governor came back after a return to Persia, he found
the works of agriculture and marketing freely practiced on the seventh day. The strenuous measures
of reform which he undertook seem to have been
efficacious for the time, and for the future as well.
Two and a half centuries later there were whole
companies of pious Jews who would die rather
than resist attack on the sacred day.

The rebuilding of the walls made possible also
social separation of Israel from her neighbors,
marriage with whom Malachi had so strongly condemned. Nehemiah even drove out of the community the grandson of the high priest who had
married the daughter of Sanballat the Horonite.

Wise provision against the shabby worship which
Malachi had vividly pictured was made in Nehemiah's requirement of a regular poll tax in support
of the temple worship. This he fixed at one-third
of a shekel.

Just what part Ezra the scribe played in all this
era of the renaissance of Jewish life and worship
in Jerusalem is a puzzle. The later historians who
combined Nehemiah's diary with records concerning Ezra and other documents, making the ecclesiastical history of Chronicles-Ezra-Nehemiah, placed
the ecclesiastic Ezra before the statesman Nehemiah, but all historical probability lies on the side
of Nehemiah as the pioneer and Ezra as a repre-

sentative of the movement which carried forward
to fuller development the ideals of Jewish separation, formulated by Ezekiel and capable of realization only after Nehemiah had rebuilt the walls.

While the great majority of the descendants of
the Babylonian exiles found a literal return to
Palestine undesirable, they did not give up interest
in the vision of a restored, purified, and holy state.
The work of codifying and developing ritual law,
undertaken by Ezekiel and the compilers of the
Holiness Code, continued among the priests in
Babylonia long after the temple was rebuilt. The
great results of this labor were the completion of
the priestly law book of Leviticus and the com-
mitting to writing of a considerable body of kindred
laws now found in the narrative of Exodus and
Numbers.

All of this legal material was given narrative
setting in a new, priestly history of antiquity,
parallel to the old prophetic histories, which now
existed in an interwoven narrative. This new
history began with a majestic story of creation in
which the all-powerful God of the universe, by his
spoken word, brought order and light out of chaos
and darkness. A beneficent being, he found his
creation all very good for man's abode and then
he entered upon a Sabbath of rest.

Back of this narrative lay the old Babylonian
story of creation, but all wonderfully transformed

by the idea of one God, the creator of heaven and earth, an idea which first reached full, conscious expression among the prophets of the exile. This noble account of creation, that culminated in the conception of the Sabbath as an institution observed by God himself, was followed by a barren genealogy of the ten antediluvians. The genealogy served as a connection between the creation and an account of the flood culminating in a covenant between God and Noah.

There follows a genealogy of the sons of Noah which is continued, in the line of Shem, down to Abram. A very brief account of Abram's migration leads up to the covenant of circumcision and the birth of Isaac, with whom God's covenant is to be established. Thus the priestly historians, writing in Babylonia, conceived of the covenant relation with God as having long antedated the meeting at Sinai.

These writers also thought of the most elaborate details of ecclesiastical organization and sacrificial worship as formulated in the wilderness period by Moses, so that they placed the great law codes in their narrative of the times of Moses. All this is quite contrary to the older histories of Israel and the express testimony of the eighth century prophets. It was inconceivable to the late historians, working at a time and place far separated from the continuity of the early national experience, that the glorious days of Moses could have lacked the full ritual law which seemed to them vital for the pure worship of God. They even transformed the simple tent of meeting, of which the older history spoke as pitched outside the camp, into a veritable portable temple constructed on the model of the finished sanctuary of Solomon.

This latest history with its embodied laws was taken as the basis and framework for a new compilation into which was fitted the combined Judean and Ephraimite history with which Deuteronomy had already been united by the editors of the early exile. The result of this union was the great composite history of antiquity which begins with the creation and extends down through the conquest and ideal allotment of the land, and now exists as the Books of Genesis, Exodus, Leviticus, Numbers, Deuteronomy, and Joshua.

The first five of these books, known as the Torah, "instruction" or "law," became the first canon of Hebrew Scripture with which the prophets and other writings were associated only later, and never on the same level in the general estimation of Judaism. Whether the completed Torah was already brought from Babylon to Jerusalem in the time of Nehemiah or only at a little later date, it certainly was the authoritative standard of the Judean community by about the year 400 B.C. The fact that the rival sanctuary on Mount

Gerizim, built for the grandson of the high priest whom Nehemiah "chased from him" because of his foreign marriage, had the Pentateuch would suggest that this was already adopted in Nehemiah's time.

In this post-exilic age circumstances combined to make it necessary to separate the little Judean community by the most rigid religious forms if the people and religion of Yahweh were not to be completely lost in the great mass of peoples that made up the Persian Empire. This condition of things brought it about that the formal, legal side of religion almost completely obscured the great significance of the prophets. We have traced the progress from primitive childlike ideas of a god who works with material, like a human artificer, who is the god of a tribe or people, to the conception of the creator of heaven and earth. We have seen this a long upward struggle, in which a succession of great prophets participated with the devotion of their lives to the new truth which it was given them to see.

To all this the men of the post-exilic age were quite blind. They had come to think of God as acting by fiat and so as revealing his perfect will for man in law rather than through such experiences as those by which Hosea and Jeremiah had come to know God. When the supreme teacher spoke in Galilee, he taught that God's revelation could not come through unconditional fiat, but must be progressive, limited by man's capacity. Nevertheless, speaking broadly, the conception of revelation which characterized the Jewish priests in Babylonia in the fifth century before Christ continued to control Christian as well as Jewish thinking until men in the nineteenth century began to recognize that, in the divine plan of life, all things unfold slowly and through struggle.

Events subsequent to the adoption of the Torah tended to stamp legalism still more firmly upon Judaism. After the Persian Empire passed under Macedonian rule through the conquests of Alexander, Greek colonies were established in Palestine as throughout his eastern dominions. Now Judaism, already marked by its distinctive and exclusive character, came into daily contact with that other most vital and persistent civilization, Hellenism. In time athletic contests and such gay religious festivals as those of Dionysus drew the young priests and others from the worship of the sanctuary and threatened the moral standards of Judaism, much as the worship of the baals and foreign deities had done in the days of their fathers.

The Jews became divided into the Hellenizers at one extreme, men who favored adoption of Greek customs and general assimilation with the rest of the empire, and the Hasidim at the other extreme, the party of the pious who were willing to die for the maintenance of the rigid standards of their law. Under Alexander's unworthy successors in Syria the high priesthood was awarded by the king to the highest bidder. At length one king, Antiochus Epiphanes, undertook to Hellenize the Jews by force. He made it a capital offense to own a copy of the Law or to circumcise a child. He caused an altar of Zeus to be erected on the altar of Yahweh in the temple court and had swine's flesh offered upon it; all were required, too, to participate in sacrifices to the Greek gods. The Hasidim refused to obey and were martyred with great cruelty; a large company who had fled and hidden in a cave met their death unresistingly because they would not defend themselves on the Sabbath.

Out of persecution sprang, at length, armed revolt. Under the leadership of Judas Maccabeus and his brothers, who survived him in the prolonged stuggle, little Judah gained independence, which she retained for nearly a century, until the coming of Pompey in 63 B.C. In this period of independence the party of the Hasidim came to be known as the Pharisees, that is, perhaps, separatists. Some of the liberal tendencies of the Hellenizers were perpetuated in the party of the Sadducees, which came to include the chief priests and their followers, while in other respects they were more conservative than the Pharisees. For

example, they considered the authoritative revelation of the law as given once for all in the Pentateuch, and refused to recognize the Pharisees'
oral development of the law, which came to be the
tradition of the elders referred to in Mark 7:3.

The leaders of the Pharisees sought with pathetic
devotion to carry out the will of God as prescribed
in his law. Since their ideal of religion was the
perfect observance of a perfect law that expressed
the will of God for man, they must determine in
every act of life just how the law was to be
applied. Hence the schools of the rabbis, or
teachers, were occupied with endless discussion of
the application of the laws to this or that conceiv-
able situation.

The field of Pharisaic discussion which is of
most general interest to us is that of Sabbath
observance. The law that no work shall be done
on this day offers difficulties that must be reckoned
with by those who purpose to carry out the law
to the letter. In time the discussions of the schools
were embodied in the Talmud, the "instruction."
In this great collection of writings the discussion
of what constitutes forbidden work upon the
Sabbath fills a considerable volume.

The Sadducees, who were not troubled with
scrupulous anxiety to observe the law perfectly,
found this additional material quite superfluous
and the law of the Pentateuch all-sufficient.

Jesus, who saw in the whole conception of religion as law the nemesis of life, showed in scathing words the evil and folly of a legalism that patiently tithed garden herbs and neglected the weightier matters of justice, mercy, and faith.

SUPPLEMENTARY READING

Peake, *The Religion of Israel*, pp. 125–37.
Addis, *Hebrew Religion*, pp. 254–306.
Ottley, *The Religion of Israel*, pp. 127–51.
Cheyne, *Jewish Religious Life after the Exile*, pp. 1–81.
H. P. Smith, *The Religion of Israel*, pp. 211–39.
Peters, *The Religion of the Hebrews*, pp. 316–20, 327–28, 338–424.
Marti, *Religion of the Old Testament*, pp. 190–237.

CHAPTER XI

THE TWO HOPES

References for study—

   (1) Amos 5:18; Hos. 11:8; 3:1–5; Isa. 7:3; Jer. 32:15.
   (2) Ezek. 34:11–31.
   (3) Isa. 9:2–7; 11:1–10; Mic. 5:2–4; Jer. 23:5–8.
   (4) Ezek. 36:32–36; 37:24–28; 38:14—39:11, 21–24; Joel 2:28–32; 3:9–21; Zech. 13:7—14:19.
   (5) Dan., chap. 7.
   (6) I Sam. 28:7–19.
   (7) Job 14:13–15; 19:25–27; Eccles. 3:19–22; 9:5, 10; Dan. 12:2–3.

Note in (1) the people's expectation in the time of Amos, the grounds of Hosea's hope, and the hope of Isaiah and Jeremiah; in (2) the shepherds, era of peace and fruitfulness; in (3) the character and work of the ideal Davidic prince; in (4) the motive for restoring Israel and the picture of distress, judgment, and prosperity; in (5) the succession of kingdoms, one like a son of man, the kingdom of the saints; in (6) the primitive idea of the future state; in (7) affirmations and denials of a future life.

At the opening of the Christian era two great hopes characterized the religion of Israel—the hope of the messianic kingdom for the nation and the hope of the resurrection for the individual. The Pharisees' exacting effort to do the will of God

as it was prescribed in the law was stimulated by
the belief that if the law could once be kept perfectly by the nation, then the messianic age would
come. If we turn back in thought to a time 750
years before the opening of the Christian era, we
find Amos picturing the people as already eagerly
expecting the day of the Lord, believing that
Yahweh was well pleased with his people and was
shortly to give them even greater triumph than
they were then enjoying. Amos and his successors labored to teach that, whatever their worship, a people could not receive the divine blessing
without being morally righteous. The Deuteronomic law partly reinforced this lesson, and the
exile destroyed the old, light-hearted confidence
in Yahweh as bound, in the nature of things, to
fight for Israel.

It was, however, the prophets with the clearest
vision of the people's blindness and perversity
who hoped that after judgment would come
restoration. Hosea saw the unchanging love of
God and knew that he could not completely cast
off his people; there must be purification through
restraint, but God's love could not be changed.
Even if those critics are right who ascribe to a later
hand the vision of the day when Israel shall return
and seek Yahweh their God and David their king,
the root of this hope lies in Hosea's vision of the
divine heart. Isaiah combined his message of

doom and hope in the name given his son, "A-remnant-shall-return." Jeremiah, who foretold the speedy destruction of Jerusalem and the temple, foresaw the day of restoration when houses and fields and vineyards should again be bought in the land.

When the city had fallen and the exiles in Babylon, who had expected far more speedy restoration than such clear-visioned prophets as Jeremiah and Ezekiel could predict, were in despair, Ezekiel drew for them a wonderful picture of Yahweh himself, their shepherd, searching for the scattered sheep, binding up the broken and strengthening the sick among them. Since here-tofore the fat and strong had shouldered away the lean and sick from pasture and water, Yahweh promised to set over them as shepherd his servant David, he himself to be their God and his servant David to be prince among them.

The character and work of the expected ruler on David's throne are beautifully pictured also in the Books of Isaiah, Jeremiah, and Micah. Since these passages usually come in awkwardly in their context and seem sometimes to have the scattering of the exile as their background, it may be that they were added to the original books of the pre-exilic prophets by later hands. In any case, from the time of Ezekiel onward Israel has embodied in her prophetic literature ideal pictures of the prince whose rule shall far surpass in its spiritual aspects the actual reign of David.

The coming ruler is to be Prince of Peace, establishing the Kingdom with justice and right- eousness, while the armor of the armored man and the garments rolled in blood shall be for fuel of fire. Upon him shall rest the spirit of Yahweh, the spirit of wisdom, and the fear of God. His judg- ments shall be rendered, not according to external appearances, but with righteousness shall he judge the poor and the meek; so there shall be peace with the earth full of the knowledge of God as the waters cover the sea. Sprung from the least of the clans of Judah, he shall be great unto the ends of the earth. When the people dwell safely in his days, remembrance of the great deliverance from exile shall replace the appeal to the deliverance from Egypt.

This group of prophets pictures national peace and world-blessing under the ideal prince of David's line, brought about by clear-visioned justice and protection for the poor and weak. In sharpest contrast stands another group of writings whose roots go back to the early prophets, though their picture is first clearly drawn in chapters 38 and 39 of Ezekiel.

The priest and prophet Ezekiel was a man of many sides in an era of transition; he combined both the priestly and the prophetic heritages of the past and looked out into the future through more than one window of the soul. In the previous chapter we saw him inspiring and shaping the ritual development of Judaism for all the centuries to follow; in this we have seen him the true prophet, with epoch-marking vision of God himself as the great tender shepherd and of the need of a righteous ruler at the head of the civil state. This state is no priestly hierarchy either. In chapter 36 he speaks from a very different point of view, as the interpreter of a God who acts for the restoration of his name that has been dishonored among the nations, and in chapter 37 he combines this motive of restoring the glory of the dishonored name with the fine vision of the Davidic shepherd and prince.

Various references in the songs and oracles of the exile make it clear that one of the hardest things for the loyal followers of Yahweh to endure was the taunting cry of their exulting enemies, "Where is now thy god?" To the mass of Israel herself the capture and destruction of Jerusalem seemed the defeat of their god, not strong enough to maintain his citadel against the gods of Babylonia. Jeremiah and Ezekiel had labored ceaselessly to forestall this danger, but with only partial success. To the minds of Israel's neighbors the fall of Jerusalem was capable of no other interpretation than that Yahweh was powerless.

Out of this situation Ezekiel's faith grew that his God must vindicate his power among the nations. This faith shaped such prophecies as we have been considering and also his expectation that there must be a great spectacular vindication of Yahweh's power. For this the distant nations were to be gathered together to overwhelm the restored Jerusalem, when they should be suddenly cut off with a destruction unprecedented in the wars of human armies. The details of the picture may have been furnished, in part, by Isaiah's ideal description of the approach of the Assyrian army as a mighty giant, striding down the summit of the mountain chain to the very outskirts of Jerusalem, there to be suddenly struck down, and in part by Zephaniah's and Jeremiah's imagery of the mysterious foe from the north that reflected the Scythian invasion of their day.

Although Ezekiel had thus at hand materials for the shaping of his conception of the great day of the future, the generalized picture is distinctly his own, and it has scarcely less influence on the future development of his people than his ideal of the restored temple and worship. It becomes the model and inspiration of a new kind of literature, the apocalypse, or revelation. By the opening of the Christian era this had become, it would seem, quite the most popular literary form in Palestine, where it played its part in kindling those

hopes that broke out in the desperate rebellions
against Rome of 66 and 132 A.D.

Adopted by the Christians, this literary form
entered the New Testament and has proved a
prolific source of much misinterpretation of Christianity, and some pathetic experiences, when men
have supposed that from it they could read the
time-table of the future and have acted on this
faith.

In the Old Testament we find brief apocalyptic
sections in Joel and in the latter part of Zechariah,
where Ezekiel's picture of the nations, gathered
together against Jerusalem that they may there
be struck down by Yahweh's power, is repeated.
The one great example of an apocalyptic book
which was included in the Old Testament is the
Book of Daniel.

Outside of the Biblical canon apocalypses or
fragments of apocalypses, ascribed to various
ancient worthies, such as Enoch, Moses, Baruch,
Ezra, have been preserved. In general these were
written during the three centuries from 200 B.C.
to 100 A.D. Their most noticeable characteristic
is the giving of an account of history, under fan-
tastic symbolism, from some earlier time down to
the period of the writer. The history is often
conceived under artificial schemes of arrangement
and is told by Enoch, or some other mouthpiece,
in the form of visions of the future. The history,

despite the symbolism and artificial conceptions, is usually intelligible to us from our general knowledge of the events, gained from other sources. As the history approaches the time of the writer, it often grows more minute in its knowledge of details, then it suddenly ceases to follow the actual course of events and passes into pictures of the great deliverance which do not accord with history.

Written in times of distress, the books have their vital purpose in expressing the undying faith of the true believers in Yahweh that his power and purpose were sufficient for his people, and in stimulating them to endure through every vicissitude.

The Book of Daniel may serve as a type of all. An ancient hero placed in the exile period is taken as the mouthpiece of one who writes from those days of distress when the temple was desecrated, with the abomination of desolation, an altar of Zeus (1 Macc. 1:54), standing upon its great altar of Yahweh. Antiochus Epiphanes has taken away the continual burnt-offering and the place of the sanctuary is cast down. The visions of successive world-kingdoms carry history down from the time of the exile to the period of this persecution; the Maccabean rebellion has already broken out, but the cleansing and rededicating of the temple by Judas Maccabeus, in the year 165 B.C., has not yet occurred.

In this time of uncertainty the apocalypse strengthens the hands of the faithful by its hope of the coming of the Ancient of Days who gives the Kingdom to the saints of the Most High. There is no word at this time of a Prince of the house of David, but one like unto a Son of Man comes with the clouds of heaven, and unto him is given the Kingdom, that all the nations and languages should serve him.

The different apocalyptic writers vary greatly in their conception of the Deliverer and the coming Kingdom of the saints. In the various apocalypses ascribed to Enoch the variation is well exhibited; in one, God himself introduces the Kingdom with no associate; in a second a superior human being appears and the people are transformed into his likeness; in a third a pre-existent being styled Righteous One, Elect One, Son of Man, Messiah, comes with the Head of Days, sits on the throne of his glory, and slays all the sinners by the word of his mouth. In one case the Kingdom is established on earth; in another it seems to be in a new heaven with the former heaven destroyed; in yet another the scene of the Kingdom is a new heaven and a new earth.

Ordinarily in the visions of this age the saints or righteous to whom the Kingdom is given are those who are faithful to the ritual law of Israel. Sometimes there is hope held out for the apostate Jews, and sometimes those nations which have not been hostile to Israel are thought of as participating in the new era in a subordinate capacity. Moral qualifications for membership in the Kingdom the apocalyptic literature leaves almost unmentioned. While apocalypse was an offshoot from prophecy, it was the expression of a priestly age which had lost the prophetic passion for social righteousness, though it held firmly to the faith in a God who would do justice for his oppressed worshipers.

Following the development of Israel's great hope for the nation, we have found in some of its later expressions the thought of a Kingdom of Heaven as the ultimate goal, and so we have touched upon the other great hope of later Judaism.

When we considered in chapter i Israel's inheritance from her ancestors and early neighbors, we noted that belief in the persistence of the spirit after death seemed to lie behind early mourning customs. Such belief certainly prevailed in the ancient world of which the Hebrews were a part. Traffic with the spirits of the dead was the stock in trade of necromancers, who were denounced by the leaders of Israel's religion from an early period. The story of Saul and the witch of Endor throws much light on the early beliefs as to the nature of existence after death. Samuel is called up out of the earth, still recognizable as an old man covered with a robe. He is able to speak in tones audible to Saul and to tell him of the divine purpose, as he did when he abode on the earth's surface.

It is evident from various passages in the Old Testament that, in common with the Babylonians, the Egyptians, and the Greeks, the ancient Hebrews thought of the dead as continuing a shadowy, uneventful existence in an abode beneath the earth's surface. Of all of these peoples, in early times, the Egyptians developed the fullest and highest conception of a future life, even forming some idea of reward and penalty determined by the character of the life that had been lived on earth. Here, as in the case of the temporary Egyptian monotheism, it seems impossible to find any direct connection of source and effect between Israel's early beliefs and those of the Egyptian religion.

In the era of the great prophets these primitive beliefs in future existence drop into the background; the nation is the unit, its righteousness and purity is the ideal, its permanent possession of the land or its restoration after judgment is the hope of the future. When religion concerns itself chiefly with matters of social morality, whether in the eighth century before Christ or in the twentieth century after Christ, interest becomes largely centered in this life, and the well-being and perpetuity of the nation or other group is the focus of hope.

With the downfall of the nation we saw that Jeremiah and Ezekiel had found the individual.

Ezekiel saw the individual's responsibility and taught that he might expect justice apart from the fate of the nation. Jeremiah saw that knowledge of God must be in the heart of each if the new covenant was to come. Yet both Jeremiah and Ezekiel looked across the exile period to a restored nation, and neither thought of a future life for the individual as the goal of hope. It was not until the Persian age, when city and temple had been restored and yet the great Shepherd of the sheep had not appeared to deliver the weak from the strong and to appoint his servant David to feed the flock, that the thought of a possible solution of the injustices of this life in a life after death began to appear.

The Book of Job mirrors the inner struggle of one who had learned from life that the material rewards are not always apportioned in accordance with the relative merits of men. In suffering of mind, body, and estate the hero of the poem longs for release in the oblivion of Sheol. Suddenly there comes to him a question in sharpest contrast to the hope of oblivion to which he has repeatedly turned: "If a man die shall he live again?" If he could believe that, he could endure all the days of his warfare. It is not yet a clear, strong hope, only a glimpse of the consoling possibilities of such a faith. Later the thought returns, and now, for a moment, it becomes a conviction that after death he shall see God on his side, no longer against him as God seems to be in his present misery.

The nation's fall was necessary if the individual was to find his standing-place before God on earth; the unsatisfying restoration and long generations of subjection and disappointment were necessary if the individual was to find hope of a life beyond, where wrong might be righted.

When Ecclesiastes was written, in the Greek period, faith in the heavenly destination of the human spirit had become so far prevalent that the writer is led to dispute the doctrine. At the opening of the Maccabean era the writer of the Book of Daniel has reached assurance of a future resurrection to everlasting life or to shame, when they that are wise "shall shine as the brightness of the firmament and they that turn many to righteousness, as the stars forever and ever."

A few late psalms are commonly interpreted as expressing a definite expectation of a resurrection, but the Old Testament was already completed before this great hope of later Judaism had come to be a prominent part of religious faith. In one of the apocalypses of Enoch, coming from Maccabean times, a clear doctrine of reward and punishment in heaven and hell first appears in Jewish literature.

Even in the first century of the Christian era both the New Testament and Josephus show the two great parties of the Jewish people divided on the question of a resurrection. The Pharisees believe, but the conservative Sadducees will have none of this new doctrine. With the destruction of Jerusalem the party of the Sadducees disappears and faith in the resurrection, with the other beliefs of the Pharisees, becomes the recognized doctrine of Jewry.

The cultured Jews of Alexandria, before and during the time of Christ, developed the rather crude resurrection faith of their Palestinian contemporaries, in the light of the Platonic conception of the soul, into a genuine doctrine of the immortality of the soul.

SUPPLEMENTARY READING

Peters, *The Religion of the Hebrews*, pp. 425–63.
H. P. Smith, *The Religion of Israel*, pp. 240–49, 293–314.
Robinson, *The Religious Ideas of the Old Testament*, pp. 184–211, 91–101.

CHAPTER XII

ISRAEL'S CONTRIBUTION TO UNIVERSAL RELIGION

It would be a serious mistake to conclude from our study of the predominant tendencies of post-exilic Judaism that all religious life had come to flow in two or three narrow channels. The charming story of Ruth, probably written during the reforms of Nehemiah and Ezra, shows that not all could sympathize with the rigid separation of Israel from her neighbors demanded by strict legalism. This is the narrative of a more spacious time, when Hebrews might intermarry with Moabites without offense and with the happiest results.

The psalms of the Persian, Greek, and Maccabean periods reflect a many-sided religious life of great depth and beauty. The reflective thought embodied in the various sections of the Book of Proverbs shows that not all the teachers of Israel were absorbed in religious institutions and ritual; there was a distinct class of teachers, "the wise," who frequented the haunts of men like the philosophers of ancient Greece. They occupied themselves with shrewd observations upon the practical results of human conduct, and endeavored to win

young men away from the paths of dissipation
and all folly to a life of self-directed industry
and continence.

The singular little story of Jonah carries us to
a broader and loftier level than any of these, even
to the thought of God's unlimited mercy, ready to
reach out to the most cruel city of which Israel
had any knowledge, in complete compassion—he
ought to spare Nineveh, in which were more than
sixscore thousand persons who could not discern
between their right hand and their left hand.

These and other currents of thought we may
discern in the varied literature of post-exilic
Judaism without going beyond the limits of the
Old Testament. If we pass on to the pre-Christian
Palestinian writings, outside of the Jewish canon,
we find, in addition to the apocalypses, stirring
history in I Maccabees, shot through with vital
religious faith and purpose no less inspiring than
the spirit of the Books of Samuel. The attractive
stories of Judith and Tobit unite religious enthusiasm with the charm of well-told tales. Tobit
gives the negative form of the golden rule, "What
thou thyself hatest, do to no man" (Tob. 4:15).

From the times after the Roman conquest there
have been preserved hymns of faith and devotion in
the so-called Psalms of Solomon. Here the old hope
of a ruler of the line of David, whose government
shall be holy, wise, just, is seen to be still burning.

Under the traditional dating of the Old Testament books and the theory that the divine revelation was limited to just those books which were finally included in the Palestinian and Christian canon of Scripture, the period from about 400 B.C. to the opening of the Christian era was conceived as four centuries of silence. We now find these centuries filled with voices that show a rich and varied religious experience continuing in Palestine, despite and often because of untoward outward circumstances.

Not all the Jews of Jesus' day were typical and confirmed Pharisees or Sadducees, else whence the companies of sympathetic followers? He deliberately disappointed the expectations of the apocalyptic messianic age; he flouted some of the most sacred institutions of the Pharisees; he taught the life of the spirit and eternal salvation which the Sadducees denied. Yet he found a considerable company who were devoted followers to the end, and a few weeks after his death thousands of the Jewish nation had become his avowed adherents.

There were, then, many among the Jewish people ready to adopt a religion of the most exacting moral and spiritual requirements, very different from the standards most insisted upon by the scribes. These facts should not be overlooked when we attempt to sum up the permanent contributions of the religion of ancient Israel.

Religion has to do with the relation of God and man so that the character of any religion is determined by its conception of God, of man, and of their connection. With these three aspects of the Hebrew religion our study has concerned itself, and under these three heads we may sum up our results in an effort to appreciate Israel's contribution to universal religion.

Through a period of twelve hundred years we have traced the main features of Israel's idea of God, from the time when he was thought of as a local deity, dwelling in the thunder clouds that wreathed the summit of a mountain, known only to a few nomad tribes. In the deliverance and covenant we found the roots of the idea that this God was himself an ethical being and that Israel's relations with him involved moral standards on her part.

Like all periods of transition to more complex civilization, the change from nomad life to settled agricultural conditions involved grave dangers for Israel, not the least of which was the adoption of the agricultural gods of Canaan. The struggle over this issue was prolonged through several centuries, during which the idea of Israel's God was expanded to include the functions of the Canaanite baals in providing the corn and the wine of the people. From time to time various political influences tended to introduce the worship of foreign deities alongside that of Yahweh or in displacement of it. The struggle involved in both of these issues tended to fix the idea that Yahweh belonged exclusively to the land of Palestine and the people of Israel, and they to him.

It was a great and difficult step to develop the simple idea of a nomad god, recognized by a small confederation of tribes, to the more complex functions of the deity of an agricultural and mercantile nation and to transfer his sphere of influence to the land of Canaan. The very things necessarily insisted upon in this transfer fixed certain ideas in a way that made further development in Israel's apprehension of God difficult. Throughout the entire period of the monarchy the mass of the people did not get beyond the idea of a national god, and they were always in danger of recognizing the gods of their neighbors in addition to their own deity.

It was in the growth of the ethical interpretation of Yahweh that the great prophets, seeking to understand the complex movement of nations, came to see the moral necessity for one God controlling these movements, not in the interest of one nation, but in the interest of justice and mercy toward all. Approach it as we may, in the last analysis it is man's moral nature through which he comes to know the one God. It was because Amos loved justice that he first came to see clearly the God of nations; it was because Hosea loved unselfishly that he first came to see the God of unchangeable love.

The downfall of the nations was required to bring to conscious expression the vital faith that the individual man is the object of the divine justice and love. Nothing less than exile in a distant land, a land whose civilization was already old when Israel became a nation, where the heavens above had been mapped from of old, and whose gods had been honored from the dawn of history—nothing less than this experience was the condition of bringing to full expression faith in the one Creator of heaven and earth.

More than six centuries separate Sinai and Babylon, Moses and the Great Unknown. Those centuries saw the development, through the succession of the prophets, of the idea of one God, Creator and Preserver, just and merciful, controlling the affairs of men in the movement of nations and in the fate of individuals. In those centuries there were developed to completion the broad outlines of the idea of God which are still the basis of the religion of Israel and of the two great religions which have sprung from the Hebrew faith.

Of the three religions which have spread widely through the world, overleaping national and racial boundaries, Buddhism, Mohammedanism, and Christianity, two rest ultimately upon faith in the

existence of the God whose nature and character
were progressively revealed in Israel within the
centuries from 1200 to 500 B.C., and the third is
found wanting as a universal religion especially
at this point—a definite conception of a personal
God.

During the five centuries that followed the exile
circumstances tended to obscure the universal idea
of God, bought with such a price, and to bring
back the old, popular idea of a god belonging
peculiarly to Israel or to the faithful remnant of
Israel. It would seem that the Jews who were
scattered abroad, mingling in the life of Babylonia
or Egypt, were able to preserve larger and nobler
ideas of God than those living in the tiny community of Judea, now just a little area about
Jerusalem. Here, though the larger conception
of the great prophets was never wholly lost, all
energies needed to be centered on keeping alive
and uncontaminated the visible worship of the
God not made with hands. It is not strange that
he came to be thought of sometimes as little more
than the champion of this small group whom he
must preserve and whose glory he must restore in
order that his own name might not perish from the
earth.

Ideas of the nature of God and the nature of
man are always interdependent, and this interde-
pendence can be clearly traced in the history of

Israel's religion. At the basis of that religion lay an act of deliverance demanding gratitude and a contract demanding fidelity. In the religion's inception justice was dispensed between man and man in the name of God. In the conflict with baalism debasing license on the one hand and control of the appetites on the other were ever in the issue.

At the time of the nation's birth supine yielding to foreign overlords or patriotic union and resistance had to be chosen, and loyalty to Yahweh was the great rallying-cry to manly action. When the nation was divided, the preservation of long-accustomed right or the yielding to despotism and forced labor was a part of the issue, and the prophet of Yahweh stood for the rights of the people. When the contest with Phoenician baalism arose, the ancient rights of the common people were again threatened by despotic ideals, and the prophet Elijah defended the rights of the small landowners against the king.

In the next century national expansion had given opportunity for one class in the community to take cruel and unfair advantage of another class. In this situation the rights of the common people were made the one supreme demand of God in a way that has made the words of Amos, Isaiah, and Micah come ringing down the ages and will make them sound on until society shall be organized,

in some way, upon a basis of economic justice, with
protection for the weak from the strong and ruthless.

The relation of nation with nation, as involving
moral standards, was hardly less prominent in the
words of Israel's great teachers than the moral
obligation of class to class. Starting with ideals
of merciless conquest which must ever prevail
when the nation is thought of as the peculiar and
especial care of its god, the prophets came to understand that, if justice is with God, governments
must deal justly in their relations with one another.

A genuine faith in a moral God of nations
involves a true internationalism. The ideal of
international union by voluntary federation rather
than by conquest has recently been traced back
to the glorious conception found in the Book of
Isaiah—Egypt and Assyria at peace, with Israel
a blessing in their midst, through the common
loyalty of all to the one God of the whole earth.
Since the day of that concrete picture, empires
have continued to be built through conquest, and
never till recent generations have experiments in
voluntary federation of peoples, united through
common ideals, not seeking aggression, been attempted on any such scale as pictured in Isaiah.
Now at last, after all these centuries, out of the
boiling cauldron of world-conflict, practical men
are seeking ways and means for the realization of
the prophet's dream for humanity.

Israel's ideal for man was one that included more than these things. It was an ideal which could never be satisfied by a righteous economic order or a righteous international system. Hosea knew better than to stop there; he saw that life's solution lies within the heart of man and that only as men come to know the God of limitless mercy can they reach their destiny. Jeremiah saw that there must be the response of the individual heart to the divine heart; that no merely national covenant was safe unless its provisions were written in the hearts of the separate members of the nation, from the least of them even unto the greatest of them.

The author of the poem on the Suffering Servant had learned the deepest lesson of all life— the truth that one being can draw another upward only as the one is willing to be despised and rejected, smitten for the sins of others.

At length some of Israel's seers learned that man's full destiny could not be attained in this house of flesh, and came to conceive the individual life in terms more worthy of its capacity, as capable of continuance in higher fulfilment beyond.

Leaders of thought in the present generation are at last apprehending the social message of the religion of Israel; but we listen long and hear faint echo in our generation of the higher truth of Hosea, Jeremiah, and the Suffering Servant, or of the hope of the fulfilment of life in the hereafter.

Such were some aspects of Israel's conception
of God and man which make her writings an ever-
new revelation of the nature of God and of the
possible destiny of man; but high and true conceptions of God and man do not of themselves make
a religion, for religion involves conscious relation
between God and man.

Human relations are maintained through various
forms of intercourse; it may be the ordinary intercourse of business and social life; it may be the
sharing of the deepest things of the soul in private
converse, public address, or written book, or
through the medium of music and art, or, again,
through carrying out the purposes of another.
Similarly men seek to maintain relations with their
gods by various forms of intercourse and expression.

Israel inherited a simple sacrificial system, rest-
ing largely on the idea of sharing with the tribal
god at the communal meal.   In Canaan they came
to recognize their God as the giver of all the
bounties of crops and fields, and to honor him with
varied offerings at different stated feasts.   Ready
to devote the most precious to him, they were
taught that he did not desire the bloody offering
of human life such as their neighbors were wont
to make.

The sacrificial ritual assumed more and more
elaborate detail, but whether the offerings were
thought of in the primitive way, as a social meal

with the Deity, or as gratitude for blessing, or
acknowledgment of sin that must be expiated at
cost, mere sacrifices were not the only means of
intercourse with the Deity; the less material
expression of the heart in prayer and in music and
song was early a part of the attempt to maintain
deep and true relations with God.

In their zeal for the recognition of God's moral
character through carrying out his moral purposes
the ethical prophets poured scorn on all sacrifice
or hymn, yet their followers saw the need of visible
means of intercourse with the Unseen and formulated a purified worship, through which the very
ethical principles of the prophets might in part be
expressed.

Personal converse, in which God spoke to the
heart of the prophet and the prophet answered
from the heart, was the basis of the higher prophetic religion. Jeremiah, especially, has permitted us to know the details of his intercourse
with his God, to whom he went with every anxiety
and complaint and in whom he found consolation
when he stood alone among his own kindred and
familiar friends.

We may find the elaborate formal worship of
post-exilic Judaism tending to defeat its own ends,
by its very elaborateness and formality putting
God far off from man; but as students of the history
of Israel's religion we may not overlook the fact

that through this rigid worship and men's uttermost devotion to its maintenance, loyalty to the God not made with hands, eternal in the heavens, was preserved through long centuries of disappointment. These apparently sterile centuries had their own part to fulfil in bringing in the fulness of time when one might declare, "Neither in this mountain, nor in Jerusalem, shall ye worship the Father. God is a Spirit; and they that worship him must worship in spirit and truth." Now, at last, the unseen God was made visible to man in the person of his Son, and the hour was come when the faith which had been developed and sheltered at Jerusalem should be spread throughout all the world.

SUPPLEMENTARY READING

Peake, *The Religion of Israel*, pp. 157–69.
Ottley, *The Religion of Israel*, pp. 202–18.
Robinson, *The Religious Ideas of the Old Testament*, pp. 212–35.
J. M. P. Smith, *The Prophet and His Problems*, pp. 209–33.
Marti, *Religion of the Old Testament*, pp. 238–51.

APPENDIX I

REFERENCE LITERATURE

The books named for supplementary reading, at the close of each chapter of the present volume, include most of the more recent works in English on the history of Hebrew religion. Of these the latest and most adequate are: J. P. Peters, *The Religion of the Hebrews* (Boston: Ginn & Co., $2.75); H. P. Smith, *The Religion of Israel*, (New York: Scribner, $2.50).

Briefer histories adapted to the uses of beginners are: A. S. Peake, *The Religion of Israel* (London: T. & E. C. Jack, 1s.); W. E. Addis, *Hebrew Religion* (New York: Putnam, $1.50); R. L. Ottley, *The Religion of Israel* (New York: Macmillan, $1.00); K. Marti, *Religion of the Old Testament* (New York: Putnam, $1.25), gives an interesting sketch of the subject drawn in broad outline.

K. Budde, *Religion of Israel to the Exile*, and T. K. Cheyne, *Jewish Religious Life after the Exile* (New York: Putnam, $1.50 each), are volumes in the series of "American Lectures on the History of Religion" and present scholarly discussions in a form adapted to a general audience.

L. B. Paton, *The Early Religion of Israel* (Boston: Houghton Mifflin Co., 50 cents), is a valuable, concise discussion of the early part of the history. J. M. P. Smith, *The Prophet and His Problems* (New York: Scribner, $1.25), is an important study of the development of the prophetic side of Hebrew religion. This is chiefly emphasized also in W. F. Badè, *The Old Testament in the Light of To-Day* (Boston: Houghton Mifflin Co., $1.75).

The article on "Religion of Israel" by E. Kautzsch, in the Extra Volume of Hastings' *Dictionary of the Bible*, and the little volume by H. W. Robinson on *The Religious Ideas of the Old Testament* (New York: Scribner, 75 cents), do not lend themselves to division so that references to them can be given at the end of each chapter, but they may well be read in connection with the study of this volume. Parts of Montefiore's *Origin and Growth of Religion as Illustrated by the Religion of the Ancient Hebrews* are still of interest. In connection with chaps. i and ii Breasted's *Development of Religion and Thought in Ancient Egypt;* S. I. Curtiss, *Primitive Semitic Religion To-Day;* and Robertson Smith, *Religion of the Semites*, and, with chap. iii, S. A. Cook, *Religion of Ancient Palestine*, will be found helpful.

The general development of Hebrew life, including religion, is treated in such histories as: C. F. Kent and J. S. Riggs, *A History of the Hebrew and Jewish People* (New York: Scribner, 4 vols., $1.25 each); H. P. Smith, *Old Testament History* (New York: Scribner, $2.50); I. J. Peritz, *Old Testament History* (New York: Abingdon Press, $1.50); F. K. Sanders, *History of the Hebrews* (New York: Scribner, $1.00); G. W. Wade, *Old Testament History* (New York: E. P. Dutton & Co., $1.50); R. Kittel, *History of the Hebrews* (to the exile only) (London: Williams & Norgate, 2 vols., 10s. 6d. each).

The history of Hebrew literature, including some discussion of its religious content, is treated in H. T. Fowler, *A History of the Literature of Ancient Israel* (New York: Macmillan, $2.25). The structure, date, and contents of the various Old Testament books are discussed in: S. R. Driver, *An Introduction to the Literature of the Old Testament* (New York: Scribner, $2.50); C. H. Cornill, *Introduction to the Canonical Books of the Old Testament* (New York: Putnam, $3.00); W. H. Bennett and W. F. Adeney,

A Biblical Introduction (New York: Thomas Whittaker, $2.00); J. E. McFadyen, *Introduction to the Old Testament,* (New York: A. C. Armstrong & Son, $1.75); G. B. Gray, *A Critical Introduction to the Old Testament* (New York: Scribner, 75 cents); G. F. Moore, *The Literature of the Old Testament* (New York: Henry Holt & Co., 50 cents). A translation of the Biblical books, analyzed into their component documents, is given in C. F. Kent, *The Student's Old Testament* (New York: Scribner, 6 vols., $2.75 per volume).

The non-canonical Jewish literature is published in R. H. Charles, *The Apocrypha and Pseudepigrapha* (Oxford: Clarendon Press, 2 vols., $21.75). The most important pseudepigrapha for the present study may be obtained separately: R. H. Charles, *The Book of Enoch* (New York: Henry Frowde, $4.00); H. E. Ryle and M. R. James, *Psalms of the Pharisees, or Psalms of Solomon* (New York: Macmillan, $3.75).

The history of Israel's ethical thought, which forms so large a part of her religion, is given in: H. G. Mitchell, *The Ethics of the Old Testament* (The University of Chicago Press, $2.00); Archibald Duff, *The Theology and Ethics of the Hebrews* (New York: Scribner, $1.25).

APPENDIX II

OUTLINE FOR STUDENTS' HISTORY

As indicated in the Preface, it is suggested that students put the results of their study of the biblical references, the text of the present volume, and supplementary readings into definite constructive form by writing a short history of the Hebrew religion. As an aid in this the following outline is offered for an essay of twenty-three chapters. Chapters ix, xix, and xxiii are designed to be summaries of the three principal divisions of the history of Israel's religion.

I. The Place of Hebrew Religion in the History of Civilization.

II. Primitive Semitic Religion.

III. The Work of Moses.

IV. Religious Practices in the Age of Moses.

V. Adoption of the Religion of a Settled, Agricultural Life.

VI. The Work of Samuel and the Sons of the Prophets.

VII. The Work of David and Solomon.

VIII. Elijah and Baal-Worship.

IX. Hebrew Religious Development before the Writing Prophets.

X. Amos the Prophet of Justice.

XI. Hosea the Prophet of Compassion.

XII. Isaiah and the God of Nations.

INDEX

Ahab: marriage of, 56; overthrow of his dynasty an-
nounced, 58.

Amos, teachings and significance of, 71–77.

Apocalypse: origin of, 158;
great popularity of, 158 f.;
form and thought of,
159–62.

Ark of Yahweh: significance
of, 33; Song of, 33; Mosaic
origin of, 33; similar Egyptian object, 33; left at Shiloh,
42; neglect of, 42; brought
to Jerusalem, 53.

Augury, Israel's comparative
freedom from, 101 f.

Babylonia: value of inscriptions in, for Hebrew history,
3 f.; early dominance of, in
Canaan, 4; Henotheism in,
7 f.

Bedawin: intermingling of,
with agriculturists in
Canaan, 36 ff.; transition
of, to settled life, 38.

Blessing of Jacob (Gen., chap.
49), ethical element in, 59.

Budde, Carl, emphasis of,
upon covenant in Mosaic
religion, 24 f.

Canaanites: influence of, on
Israel, 39 ff., 44 f., 75; character of religion among, 40,
75; certain functions of
gods assumed by Yahweh
of, 44 f.; Hezekiah's attack

upon practices of, 100;
Manasseh's restoration of
practices of, 100 ff.; constant
influence of, before Deuteronomy, 105 f.; sweeping
away of, in Josiah's reform,
110; better elements ab-
sorbed by Yahweh worship,
110.

Central sanctuary, sacrifice
limited to, 105 f.

Child sacrifice: a Canaanite
practice, 40; traces of in
the Old Testament, 102;
relation of, to law of first-
born, 102.

Christianity, relation of, to
Hebrew religion, 1 ff., 5 f.,
81, 90, 137 f., 152, 169.

Circumcision, prevalence of,
in and near Canaan, 10.

Commandments, the Ten:
later than Moses, 28; as
given in early Judean History, 64; of Exod., chap. 20,
and Deut., chap. 5, 107.

Covenant: Budde's emphasis
upon, 24 f.; Book of (Exod.
20:22—23:19), in Ephraim-
ite history, 67; contents of,
67 f.; relation of Deuteronomy to, 105; Jeremiah's
doctrine of New, 124 f.

Daniel, Book of, 160 f.; resurrection hope in, 165.

David: founder of monarchy,
51; primitive character of
religion of, 52 f.; real

Ikhnaton: attempt of, to establish monotheism, 8; moral ideals of, 29.

Images: in early Israel, 41 f.; use of, in Hosea's time, 79, 82.

Immortality. See Resurrection.

Individualism: origin of Jeremiah's doctrine of, 118 f., 121; Ezekiel's development of doctrine of, 119 f.; relation of, to universal religion, 125.

Isaiah: life and teachings of, 86–95; the "Second Isaiah," 131–37.

Jacob, blessing of (Gen., chap. 49), 59.

Jeremiah, 114–22, 124 f.

Jerusalem: favorable situation of, 16 f.; beginning of religious importance of, 53.

Jezebel: worship of Tyrian Baal, introduced by, 56 f.; Tyrian despotism introduced by, 57 f.

Job, hope of future life in, 164.

John, Gospel of, in relation to Hosea, 81.

Jonah, lofty thought in Book of, 168.

Josiah: relation of reforms of, to Deuteronomy, 109; temporary character of reforms of, 110 ff.

Judean prophetic history: landmark in world-literature, 61 f.; religious significance of, 61–65; Decalogue of chap. 34, 64; influence of, on Deuteronomy, 104 f.

Judith, Book of, 168.

Kadesh: judicial decisions given at, 26; meaning of name, 34; center of life during wilderness period, 34 f.

Law: origin of, 77; development of, before Deuteronomy, 105 f.; code of Deuteronomy, 105–13; Holiness Code, 129 f.; emphasis on Sabbath in successive codes, 143; the priestly law, 146–49; capital offense to own a copy of the, 150; oral development of, 151. See also Commandments; Covenant, Book of.

Levites: early status of, 42; distinction between sons of Zadok and other Levites, 127 f.; status of, in Code of Deuteronomy, 128.

Leviticus, completion of, 145. See also Law.

Maccabees, Book of I, 168.

Malachi, 141 f.

Man, summary view of development of ideal of, 173–77.

Manasseh: reintroduction of Canaanite practices by, 100, 102; introduction of religious practices from Babylonia by, 100 ff.; child sacrifice of, 102 f.; relation of Deuteronomic law to, 106.

Messianic hope: in Book of Isaiah, 93 ff., 137; development of from time of Amos to post-exilic period, 154 ff.; apocalyptic forms of, 161 f.;

Handbooks of Ethics and Religion

The Spread of Christianity in the Modern World. *By Edward Caldwell Moore.* $2.50, postpaid $2.60.
A survey of the history of missions since the beginning of the modern era.

How the Bible Grew. *By Frank G. Lewis.* $1.50, postpaid $1.60.
The first single work to record the growth of the Bible from its beginning to the present time.

The Life of Paul. *By Benjamin W. Robinson.* Revised Edition. $2.00, postpaid $2.10.
This narrative furnishes a reliable guide to a study of Paul's career.

The Religions of the World. *By George A. Barton.* Revised Edition. $3.00, postpaid $3.10.
The author gives a keen and sympathetic interpretation of all the great religions of the world.

The Psychology of Religion. *By George A. Coe.* $2.25, postpaid $2.35.
Adapted for use as a college text and at the same time interesting reading for those outside of scholastic circles.

The Story of the New Testament. *By Edgar Johnson Goodspeed.* $1.00, postpaid $1.10.
A clear exposition of the development of the New Testament.

The Origin and Growth of the Hebrew Religion. *By Henry T. Fowler.* $2.00, postpaid $2.10.
A remarkable exposition of religious phenomena from a fresh psychological standpoint.

The Teaching of Jesus: A Source Book. *By Ernest D. Burton.* $3.00, postpaid $3.10.
Jesus' teaching, that of his contemporaries, and some valuable extra-gospel source material on Jewish literature of the New Testament period.

The Moral Life of the Hebrews. *By J. M. Powis Smith.* $2.50, postpaid $2.60.
A history of the development of Hebrew morals as recorded in the Old Testament.

The Rise of Christianity. *By Frederick Owen Norton.* $2.50, postpaid $2.60.
An interpretation in narrative form of the source materials for the origin and early development of Christianity.

Principles of Preaching. *By Ozora S. Davis.* $2.50, postpaid $2.60.
A new text for the student of homiletics and the preacher who desires his sermons to gain in power, persuasiveness, and beauty of form.

Principles of Christian Living. *By Gerald B. Smith.* $2.00, postpaid $2.10.
A new book on Christian ethics, designed to indicate the motives which enter into Christian living as the individual finds himself a member of various groups in everyday life.

The Prophets and Their Times. *By J. M. Powis Smith.* $2.50, postpaid $2.60.
The perennially interesting lives of the prophets reconstructed and interpreted for students of religion.

Current Christian Thinking. *By Gerald B. Smith.* $2.00, postpaid $2.10.
Mr. Smith discusses the outstanding forms of modern Christian belief.

Religious Education. *By Theodore G. Soares.* $2.50, postpaid $2.60.
A textbook for college and theological seminary courses in the fundamental principles of religious education.

Preaching on Church and Community Occasions. *By Ozora S. Davis.* $2.50, postpaid $2.60.
This book suggests subjects and ways of handling the many special-occasion sermons which the minister is called upon to give.

Character through Creative Experience. *By William C. Bower.* $2.50, postpaid $2.60.
A new ideal and a new technique for character education is formulated in this book.

THE UNIVERSITY OF CHICAGO PRESS
CHICAGO · ILLINOIS